How We Hope

How We Hope

A Moral Psychology

Adrienne M. Martin

PRINCETON UNIVERSITY PRESS
Princeton & Oxford

Requests for permission to reproduce material from this work should be sent to
   Permissions, Princeton University Press
Published by Princeton University Press, 41 William Street, Princeton, New Jersey 08540
In the United Kingdom: Princeton University Press, 6 Oxford Street, Woodstock,
   Oxfordshire OX20 1TW

press.princeton.edu

Library of Congress Cataloging-in-Publication Data

Martin, Adrienne M.
How we hope : a moral psychology / Adrienne M. Martin.
pages cm
Includes bibliographical references and index.
ISBN 978-0-691-15152-6 (hardcover : alk. paper) 1. Hope. I. Title.
BD216.M37 2013
128—dc23   2013014198

British Library Cataloging-in-Publication Data is available

This book has been composed in Adobe Garamond and Myriad

Printed on acid-free paper ∞

10 9 8 7 6 5 4 3 2 1

For Chris

Ein Yahav

A night drive to Ein Yahav in the Arava Desert,
a drive in the rain. Yes, in the rain.
There I met people who grow date palms,
there I saw tamarisk trees and risk trees,
there I saw hope barbed as barbed wire.
And I said to myself: That's true, hope needs to be
like barbed wire to keep out despair,
hope must be a mine field.

> From Yehuda Amichai, "Israeli Travel: Otherness is All,
> Otherness is Love," #7

> *Translated by Chana Bloch and Chana Kronfeld*

Table of Contents

As documented in the introduction to this book, my interest in hope began during my time as a postdoctoral fellow at the National Institutes of Health's Department of Bioethics. This was a wonderful fellowship that, in many ways, changed the way I think about all subjects. I am especially grateful to Ezekiel Emanuel and David Wendler for pushing me to take hope seriously as a topic of philosophical inquiry.

I wrote the bulk of the manuscript while on leave from the University of Pennsylvania, and during a fellowship at the Princeton University Center for Human Values. I am grateful to both institutions for their support. The Center for Human Values and connected programs and groups at Princeton provide a uniquely stimulating and supportive environment for academic research, and I am indebted to the many, many people who took an interest in my work while I was there. I particularly want to mention Anthony Appiah, Charles Beitz, Elizabeth Harman, Peter Singer, and my fellow fellows: Corey Brettschneider, Tom Christiano, Gerry Mackie, Tim Mulgan, Colleen Murphy, Jonathan Quong, and John Seery. Well after we had returned to our home institutions, Colleen and Jonathan also took the time to provide valuable comments on a complete draft of the book.

Andrew Chignell, David McNaughton, and Nancy Sherman read and commented on the entire manuscript, and the book is much improved as a result (though of course any remaining shortcomings are mine alone). Conversations with Ingra Schellenberg were important to my thoughts in chapter 3. In addition to providing helpful substantive comments, Chris Melenovsky took the mess of footnotes in an early draft and magicked them into a real set of references. He did a wonderful job preparing the index.

I have received profound support—in relation to this book project, but also more broadly in my career as a philosopher—from Cheshire Calhoun, Samuel Freeman, Maggie Little, Martha Nussbaum, and Kok-Chor Tan. I am not infrequently overwhelmed at how fortunate I am to have such generous colleagues and mentors.

Sections of the first three chapters contain revised parts of a previously published paper, "Hopes and Dreams," and I thank *Philosophy and Phenomenological Research* for the permission to use this material.

My mother, Valerie Martin, and my partner, Chris Hayes, have been my sounding boards for many years, and I doubt this book would exist without them. Finally, it does truly take a village: Megan Yancey, Ashley Mutch, Katiria Rivera, and Stephanie Roy all provided wonderful care for my beloved daughter, Calliope, during the time I was writing and revising this book.

How We Hope

What Is Hope?

Questions about Hope

I first became interested in hope as a subject of philosophical inquiry in 2004, when I took up a postdoctoral fellowship at the National Institutes of Health's Department of Bioethics, and John Kerry began his presidential campaign against George W. Bush. In my daily life, hope was simultaneously an object of such strong approval and suspicion that I began to wonder what, exactly, it is. And, once I started paying close attention to what people said about hope, when they expressed it, and when they reared back from it, I began to think there was a fair amount of confusion about it.

The Department of Bioethics is institutionally and physically inside the NIH's Clinical Center in Bethesda, Maryland, which is where the NIH's clinical researchers carry out their trials—it is a hospital where every patient is a research participant. During my two years there, I spent much of my time following a cancer investigator on his rounds with participants in two phase I trials of Avastin. A phase I trial tests an experimental drug or potential treatment for toxicity and tolerance in humans. It is not until phase II, after the tolerable maximum dosage has been determined at phase I, that researchers begin to test an experimental drug's effectiveness. The participants in phase I trials are either healthy volunteers or terminally ill patients who have exhausted the known treatments for their condition and wish to contribute to research and, perhaps, hope the experimental drug will unexpectedly benefit them. The chances of a participant in a phase I trial receiving medical benefit from the experimental drug are typically less than one percent, and participants are informed of this fact.

The participants in the trials I followed were terminally ill with forms of cancer for which Avastin was not yet approved as a treatment. Genentech (bought by Hoffmann LaRoche in 2009) makes Avastin/bevacizumab, which blocks the growth of blood vessels, including at some tumor sites. In 2004, it was first approved for use in combination with chemotherapy to treat both metastatic colorectal and metastatic small-cell lung cancer. It was, and continues to be, exorbitantly expensive, but many researchers believe it has great promise, and there are many trials seeking new applications for it.[1]

Hope was a regular topic at the meetings I attended. If the investigator reported stabilized or reduced tumor size, the participant would light up and declare, "So, there's hope!" If he reported increased tumor size, or raised reasons to think enrollment in a different trial might yield a better chance of medical benefit, the participant would, often, visibly steel him or herself and ask, "Is there still hope?" (Tumor size is one of the standard measures of a cancer drug's effectiveness, despite the research community's awareness that there is no correspondence between it and prolonged life or improved quality of life.) While the investigator never raised the topic of hope himself, the Center administrators enthusiastically embraced the unofficial name given the Center at a public event by longtime cancer research participant, Susan Butler: the "House of Hope." "Hope" was emblazoned across press releases, ads for trials, and internal emails at the Center. It would be a feat for anyone entering the Center not to see it as offering hope, and intentionally so. Indeed, this is true of the medical research industry as a whole: hope is the watchword.

The investigator's responses to these requests for hope were always measured. He feared both "taking away" hope, and generating or supporting "false hope." Many medical caregivers see this as their most difficult quandary: too much blunt forthrightness and their patients will be crushed by despair; too much optimism and their patients will feel betrayed if they do not recover as hoped—and then, again, they may be crushed by despair.

At the Clinical Center, I also regularly attended the Palliative Care team's meetings, where the team members—ranging from doctors and nurses specializing in pain medication to social workers to massage, art, and pet therapists—discussed their efforts to alleviate the suffering of some of the Center's most seriously ill patient-participants. They took a more nuanced view of hope. Most of their patients had already given up on pursuing a cure or even extended life, and turned their focus to living their final days as comfortably as possible and dying well.[2] Thus, the team members had little fear of purveying "false" hope. They did not occupy the role of someone holding out

1 In 2008, I published a paper titled "Hope and Exploitation," in which I used Genentech as an example of a company that exploits the hopes of the terminally ill by charging excessive prices for questionably effective treatments. I was particularly concerned about their marketing of Avastin for the treatment of advanced metastatic breast cancer, which the FDA approved in February of 2008, despite the Oncology Drug Advisory Committee's contrary recommendation in December 2007. Unfortunately, I was vindicated in July 2010, when the FDA revoked this approval. See Adrienne M. Martin, "Hope and Exploitation," *Hastings Center Report* 38.5 (2008): 49–55.

2 Palliative care is usually run this way—i.e., as the alternative to continued treatment, as preparation for death. Doctors often resist drawing on the resources of palliative care, because they see it as an admission of failure. This is too bad, because any patient could benefit from the forms of care I saw this thoughtful and innovative team provide.

the possibility of cure or extended life. They could focus instead on helping their patients find the most beneficial forms of hope.

As a result of my experiences in this medical setting, I formed a lot of questions about hope. Is it really the last and best bulwark against crushing despair? If so, how does it work, and how is it lost? What does it mean to say hope is "false"? Is supporting hope ever literally deceptive? What are the best forms of hope? How does hope influence deliberation and decision-making?

With my ear attuned to the rhetoric of hope, I was struck by what would otherwise have seemed the laughably trivial struggle between John Kerry and John Edwards over the slogan for their White House campaign. When Kerry accepted the Democratic nomination, his speech included the declaration "Help is on the way." Edwards, who had campaigned as a practitioner of a "politics of hope," transformed Kerry's phrase into "Hope is on the way." Some pundits criticized Edwards for this move, on the grounds that *help* is a concrete promise, while *hope* is both a vague and a naïve thing to offer. Others were moved by Edwards' hope rhetoric, finding it an uplifting clarion call to change divisive and negative Washington politics. It is noteworthy that we saw exactly the same split over Barack Obama's hope campaign in 2008: some believed it pointed up his relative youth and inexperience, and revealed him as a naïve dreamer without a concrete plan; others rallied to it as the answer needed in a time of strife. This division amplified the questions I was already entertaining, and convinced me of their interest beyond the medical arena. It also added another question to my list: How could hope seem to one person an unrealistic vagary and to another a solid anchor in a storm? I suspected this division in the political arena was due to the audience's imaginative resources—some responded to a call for hope with drifting and dreams, and others with reality-responsive plans. It was their own responses coloring their interpretation of the call. What, then, I wondered, is the connection between hope and imagination?

There are many places one can look for answers to such questions. Positive psychologists have developed several instruments intended to measure hope, and there have been numerous studies of the relation between hope so measured and both mental and physical health outcomes, as well as decision-making. Christian theologians place hope at the center of a virtuous life, and Aquinas in particular has a detailed analysis of hope. Existential philosophers see hope as an essential part of the human condition, not so much the alternative to as the natural companion of the angst and despair we feel when we confront the meaninglessness universe. For Marxist philosopher Ernst Bloch, the hope for a better life, expressed in human activities ranging from daydreams to fashion to political utopianism, is the key to discerning and dismantling ideology. The list could go on. The tradition I work in, "analytic" philosophy, has been oddly reticent about hope, and this book aims to rectify that situation. I do touch and draw on many of the sources named above, but

I believe the methods of philosophical analysis and the theories of mind and action developed within this tradition yield unique insights on the subject. I equally believe that, were analytic philosophy unable to yield unique insights on hope, it would be the worse for analytic philosophy. So this book is also a test of these methods and theories.

The Orthodox Definition and Its Critics

Within the analytic tradition, the small literature that does address hope coalesces into a definite thematic dialogue, centered on what I will call the "orthodox" definition of hope as a combination of the desire for an outcome and the belief that the outcome is possible but not certain. This definition has its roots in the early Modern period, and may be understood as a reaction against the way hope was conceived by the Scholastics—namely, as a distinctive kind of subrational motivational force. Thomas Aquinas bases his faculty psychology on that of the Platonic and Peripatetic schools. The latter distinguish between the "appetitive" and "spirited" parts of the soul, both of which are supposed to have motivational functions. Although the spirited part is supposed to "partake of" or "share in" reason in some way, it is not itself supposed to be a *rational* motivational faculty; instead, it is the rational soul's enforcer, ruling over the (also nonrational) appetites according to reason's dictates, at least when the soul is well ordered.[3] Modifying this distinction, Aquinas holds that the nonrational—or perhaps it would be more accurate to say *sub*rational—appetite has two powers: the "concupiscible" and the "irascible." The concupiscible appetite is our capacity to be attracted to the things we perceive as good, and repelled by those we perceive as bad; the irascible appetite is our capacity to strive against obstacles to our achieving the good or avoiding the bad. Hope, he argues, is an *irascible* passion.

Most Western philosophers from the sixteenth century on abandon this distinction within the appetites, proposing instead a psychology with a single subrational motivational power—call it "Desire," or "Appetite," or "Passion." This power may manifest in different ways in different epistemic circumstances. For example, it may be *fear* in the context of uncertain harm and *despair* in the context of present harm. Nevertheless, it is a single power. Of course, many rationalist philosophers during this period also propose a rational motivational power (and extreme rationalists like Spinoza make out even *desire* to be a rational power, eliminating the subrational faculties entirely). In chapter 2, I will argue that the idea that we have both subrational

---

3   Peter King, "Aquinas on the Passions," in *Aquinas's Ethical Theory: Essays in Honor of Norman Kretzmann*, Scott MacDonald and Eleonor Stump, eds. (Ithaca, NY: Cornell University Press, 1999). I go into detail about Aquinas in chapter 3.

and rational motivational powers is crucial to our understanding of hope. For now, however, the essential point of contrast is that while Aquinas and the Scholastics who followed him consider hope and desire distinct forms of sub-rational motivation, the Modern period abandons the distinction between the irascible and concupiscible passions, thereby setting the stage for analyzing hope as a specific case of desire. Thus the orthodox definition: to hope for an outcome is to desire it while believing it is possible but not certain to obtain.

Much of the contemporary literature accepts the orthodox definition as an analysis of some "lowest common denominator"[4] form of hope. On this view, the orthodox definition is true in particular of the rather trivial way we often express hope: "I hope the train comes on time"; "I hope you are well"; "I hope the weather is clear tomorrow"; and so on. I myself disagree with this conciliatory notion, and will eventually argue that the orthodox definition is inadequate to even such trivial hope. However, among those who accept the orthodox definition for lowest common denominator hopes, there is a methodology I find fruitful. This methodology is to begin an inquiry about hope by focusing on what I will call *hoping against hope,*[5] or hoping for an outcome that one highly values but believes is extremely unlikely. Hoping against hope has two features in particular that appear to elude the orthodox definition.

First, the orthodox definition strikes many as inadequate to the phenomenology of hoping against hope. When we hope against hope, overcoming our circumstance captures our attention and imagination in a way that seems to go beyond desire. As Margaret Urban Walker writes, hope is "an emotional stance or 'affective attitude,' a recognizable syndrome that is characterized by certain desires and perceptions, but also by certain forms of attention, expression, feeling, and activity."[6] When we hope, the experience often seems more profound than is typical of desire; hope seems to color our experience in a way that is both richer and more specific than does desire.

Second, it is a common pretheoretical intuition that hoping against hope has a special kind of sustaining power, that it is uniquely supportive of us in times of trial and tribulation. The orthodox definition seemingly cannot accommodate this intuition. Desiring, even desperately so, to overcome such situations doesn't have any *special* kind of motivational power. Moreover, recognizing extremely slim odds seems likely only to hold one back or make one's efforts more timid.

---

4 Phillip Pettit, "Hope and Its Place in the Mind," *Annals of the American Academy of Political and Social Science* 592 (2004): 152–65.

5 Some people tell me that, to their ear, "hoping against hope" rings of irrationality. I am assuming, however, that as I define it, it is at least not *obviously* irrational. An important part of my inquiry goes to whether and, if so, when, such hope is rational. The phrase has its origins, I believe, in St. Paul's description of Abraham as he "Who against hope believed in hope, that he might become the father of many nations" (Romans 4:18).

6 Margaret Urban Walker, *Moral Repair* (Cambridge: Cambridge University Press, 2006), 48.

Of course, both of these claims about the orthodox definition are empty without a convincing account of *desire*—the defendant of this definition may simply claim that we have underestimated desire's ability to engage our minds and feelings, or to motivate us in challenging circumstances. Indeed, in chapter 1 I will argue that, on the most widely accepted philosophical conception of desire, the orthodox definition *can* account for much of the phenomenology of hope—even hope that is "against hope." However, I will also argue that this definition is nevertheless insufficient to fully distinguish certain cases of hoping against hope. Moreover, once we add the missing element to the orthodox definition, we see that it does fall short when it comes to explicating hope's sustaining power; desire is pretty unreliable as a form of motivation, while hope has the potential to regulate our imaginative and agential activities in a steady and sustaining way. Hope truly emerges as, in Walker's words, a "syndrome" of attitudes and feelings. Once we see the fullness of hope as a syndrome, it also becomes apparent that even so-called lowest common denominator hopes are more complex than the orthodox definition would have it, even if their constituent syndromes are largely unrealized dispositions.

Hope as a Syndrome

Syndrome analyses of emotional attitudes like hope have a number of theoretical advantages. By incorporating distinct but related elements such as feelings, modes of perception and thought, and motivational states, a syndrome analysis is faithful to the sense of *richness* we associate with these attitudes. This richness can be difficult to account for, if we analyze an attitude as a belief or judgment, or a sensation, or a desire or intention, or even a combination of two or three such elements. A syndrome analysis is also rarely proposed as a set of necessary and sufficient conditions, but rather as a set of paradigmatic marks of the analysandum. Thus it can shed light on why we are sometimes ambivalent about attributing hope (or whatever attitude is under analysis) to a person. Sometimes, a person is only *partially* hopeful. Perhaps she desires an outcome and her thoughts occasionally drift to it, but she is not disposed to expend much energy or thought on its possibility; she has a fairly idle, borderline case of hope. That is, she entertains some of the elements of the syndrome, but does not hope in the fullest sense—she does not embody the full syndrome.

The danger of a syndrome analysis is that it runs the risk of being *ad hoc*. If we simply read off the elements of the purported syndrome from our observations of robust cases of hope, we have not really defined or analyzed or had an insight into hope at all. An insightful syndrome analysis must identify a *unifying element*, a part or aspect of hope that makes sense of the other constitutive elements, that truly makes hope a *syndrome* rather than a random collection of things. I dedicate the first two chapters of this book to determining what element unifies hope as a syndrome of feelings, thoughts, perceptions, and motives. Here, it may be useful to provide a sketch of the view at which I arrive. I call it the "incorporation analysis."

The Incorporation Analysis

I argue that the key to understanding hope—first hope held "against hope," and then hope more broadly speaking—is to begin with the right general theory of human motivation. I reject, first, a Humean theory, according to which all human action is the product of a single kind of nonrational motivational representation: usually called "desire" (I will ultimately prefer the term "attraction," in order to highlight the nonrational nature of the representation).[7] A second inadequate theory is a purely rationalist theory, according to which all human action is the product of a single kind of rational representation: for example, the judgment that a consideration is a reason for action.[8] I argue that we have independent reason for thinking both of these *monist* theories inadequate to the first-personal experience of deliberation and choice, whereby we seem capable of both desiring (being attracted to) an outcome and judging that desire no reason at all to pursue the outcome. Moreover, neither monistic theory can capture the difference between two people who in some sense equally desire and assign the same probability to the same outcome, and yet differ in how much they hope for it—and such cases abound. We need, instead, a *dualist* theory of motivation, according to which we are capable both of representing an outcome as *desirable* (attractive) and of representing some of the outcome's features—including our own desire for it— as providing or failing to provide *reasons* to pursue it.[9]

Once we adopt a dualist theory of motivation, we can see that hope has the following structure: to hope for an outcome is to *desire* (be attracted to) it, to

7 The Humean theory is probably the most widely-accepted philosophical theory of human motivation. Canonical expressions of this view can be found in Bernard O. Williams, "Internal and External Reasons," reprinted in *Moral Luck* (Cambridge: Cambridge University Press, 1981), 101– 13; and Michael Smith, "The Humean Theory of Motivation," *Mind* 96 (1987): 36–61. (However, see chapter 2, n.8 of this book for some reasons to doubt that Williams' argument actually supports the Humean theory.)

8 Recent proponents of the rationalist theory are T. M. Scanlon, *What We Owe to Each Other* (Cambridge, MA: Harvard University Press, 1998); and Derek Parfit, *On What Matters* (Oxford: Oxford University Press, 2011).

9 Such a dualist theory is developed by a number of prominent Kantians, especially John Rawls, *A Theory of Justice* (Cambridge, MA: Harvard University Press, rev. ed. 1999); Christine Korsgaard, in *The Sources of Normativity*, O. O'Neill, ed. (Cambridge: Cambridge University Press, 1996), and *Self-Constitution: Action, Identity and Integrity* (Oxford: Oxford University Press, 2009); and Tamar Schapiro, "The Nature of Inclination," *Ethics* 119.2 (2009): 229–56.

assign a *probability* somewhere between 0 and 1 to it, and to judge that there are sufficient *reasons* to engage in certain feelings and activities directed toward it. The element that unifies hope as a syndrome is this final element, which I argue is a way of *incorporating* hope's other elements into one's rational scheme of ends.

I develop this account in detail in chapters 1 and 2, by identifying the central feelings and activities associated with hope (chapter 1), and arguing that the rational norms governing the incorporation element of hope are exclusively *practical*—that is to say, what makes hope rational as far as this element is concerned is exclusively a matter of whether it coheres with and contributes to one's rational scheme of practical ends (chapter 2). I then spend two chapters drawing out the implications of the resulting conception of hope for hope's influence on motivation, and in particular for its purported power to sustain us in times of trial. Finally, in the last chapter, I argue that our ordinary mode of relating to each other interpersonally (and relating to ourselves intrapersonally) essentially involves a normative variation of hope. In more detail, the chapters proceed as follows.

Summary of Chapters

In chapter 1, I present a series of challenge cases for the orthodox definition, cases that show this definition cannot distinguish strong hopes for highly unlikely outcomes from either weaker hopes or even despair directed at those outcomes. To truly capture what it is to "hope against hope," we need to supplement the orthodox definition. I then consider and reject three recent proposals about how to supplement the definition. Although these three proposals—from Philip Pettit,[10] Luc Bovens,[11] and Ariel Meirav[12]—are not ultimately successful, I argue that there are important lessons we should take from each. In light of these lessons, I propose the incorporation analysis of hope, whereby hoping for an outcome is a distinctive way of treating one's own attitudes toward the outcome. Specifically, one treats them as reasons to engage in various feelings and activities, and thereby *incorporates* them into one's rational scheme of ends.

At the end of the first chapter, I characterize the activities of thought, feeling, and planning that are paradigmatic of hope. Then, in chapter 2, I further elaborate the incorporation analysis. Hope does indeed involve the basic elements of the orthodox definition—the desire for an outcome and a subjective

10 Pettit, "Hope and Its Place in Mind."

11 Luc Bovens, "The Value of Hope," *Philosophy and Phenomenological Research* 59 (1999): 667–81.

12 Ariel Meirav, "The Nature of Hope," *Ratio: An International Journal of Analytic Philosophy* 22.2 (2009): 216–33.

probability estimate between 0 and 1. In addition, hope, when most fully realized, makes use of our capacities of self-reflection and rational justification; when we hope, we treat both our desire and our probability assignment as justifying reasons for hopeful activities such as, for example, fantasizing about the hoped-for outcome. This is the feature that unifies the syndromatic elements of thought, feeling, and planning, and makes hope a distinctive and cohesive practical attitude. I argue further that the justifications to which we commit ourselves in virtue of hoping are *practical* justifications, and that there are few epistemic or theoretical limitations on rational hope. One natural worry about this analysis is that it makes hope into an overly reflective or sophisticated attitude—for example, under this analysis, it appears very young children and nonhuman animals are not capable of hope. I conclude chapter 2 by addressing this worry.

The core set of questions that sparked my interest in hope regard its role in motivation. Is it really the last, best bulwark against despair? Is inspiring hope a good way to motivate people to action? How, more generally, does hope influence deliberation and motivation? In chapter 3, I therefore turn to consider the implications of the incorporation analysis for these questions. I focus on hope in the context of a "trial"—an extreme challenge to one's ability to live well or flourish, a circumstance that makes literal or figurative suicide tempting—but my argument extends to less profound circumstances, as well. I argue that hope has the potential to influence motivation in an interesting and distinctive variety of ways, but that its influence is, for the most part, contingent: hope is not, in itself, a uniquely powerful or reliable form of sustenance. Contrary to popular opinion, whether hope is indeed a good resource in terrible circumstances is an entirely contingent matter. It is contingent on how we express our hopes, especially on how we exercise our hopeful imaginations.

The conclusion of the third chapter, that hope's ability to support us in times of trial is contingent, applies to hope in general. There is, however, a specification of hope that is both *structured* to close off suicide (literal or figurative) as an attractive option and immune to disappointment. Or so I argue in chapter 4. This specification of hope is directed at an "unimaginable" outcome, or an outcome that outstrips our available concepts and has the marks of the attitude we often call "faith." One might wonder if this is bad news for atheists. Have we lost a crucial survival tool? I argue, to the contrary, that there is such a thing as secular faith, an attitude that has the sustaining power and immunity to disappointment of religious faith, but that does not presuppose any religious commitments. There is, then, a form of hope that is a unique bulwark against despair and capable of sustaining us through trials, no matter what comes. However, though it is available to the religious and secular alike, it is quite specific, and not easily attainable. Again, then, popular appeals to hope and its value require serious qualification.

In the final chapter, I shift gears to argue that hope plays a crucial role in our standard ways of relating to each other "interpersonally" (and to ourselves intrapersonally). One way that we relate to each other interpersonally—or from what Peter Strawson dubs the "participant stance"[13]—is to hold each other responsible. This mode of interaction is best construed, I argue, as what Jay Wallace calls "normative expectation."[14] Departing somewhat from the details of Wallace's view, I argue that to *normatively expect* someone to comply with a requirement is to be prepared to justify a narrow set of "reactive" feelings: resentment, indignation, and guilt. Normative expectation and these reactive feelings are at the heart of relating to people as rational agents by holding them responsible.

What I call "normative hope" is an attitude closely related to, but distinct from normative expectation. To place *normative hope* in a person is not to hold her responsible, exactly, but it is still to relate to her as a rational agent, because it means holding up principles to her as rationally aspirational. It is to be prepared to justify feelings such as interpersonal disappointment and gratitude. When we feel gratitude for a supererogatory action, this does not reflect our normative expectation of some lesser action (though we may have this expectation); instead, it reflects our feeling that the action's principle is something to which ordinary agents need only aspire. When we feel gratitude for a dutiful action, this reflects our attitude that the target faced genuine challenges, so that dutiful action is a genuine accomplishment. When a parent feels disappointment in an errant child, this reflects his sense that the child's status as a reasoner provided a similar challenge. And, I argue, when we invest normative hope in the morally vicious, this amounts to a condemnation of their vice, as well as an aspiration on their behalf.

Hope deserves rather a different reputation than it has. On the one hand, it does not deserve a reputation as either unqualifiedly good or unqualifiedly reliable. Its relation to rational action and a good life is more complex. On the other hand, it is of far deeper philosophical interest and significance than most have recognized. It is revelatory of the structures and operations of reflective human consciousness, and it can be a strategically valuable response to the fact that we are creatures with animal attractions, with the capacity for rational deliberation and choice, and the capacity to be aware of our own epistemic and agential limitations. In the conclusion to this book, I pull together these points and outline recommendations for the philosophy of psychology and the emotions that follow from this investigation of hope.

13 P. F. Strawson, "Freedom and Resentment," in *Freedom and Resentment and Other Essays* (Abingdon, UK: Routledge, 2008).

14 R. Jay Wallace, *Responsibility and the Moral Sentiments* (Cambridge, MA: Harvard University Press, 1994).

Beyond the Orthodox Definition of Hope

Recent philosophical work on hope centers on what I will call the "orthodox" definition of hope. According to this definition, hope is a combination of the desire for an outcome and the belief that the outcome is possible
but not certain; another way to cast hope, under this definition, is as desire
in the context of epistemic uncertainty. This definition has its roots in the
early Modern period, and has both advocates and detractors among contemporary philosophers. I am among the detractors, because I think hope is
a distinctive practical attitude by which we incorporate our desires for uncertain outcomes into our agency, in a specific way. To anticipate, hoping for
an outcome involves standing ready to offer a certain kind of justificatory
rationale for engaging in certain kinds of thought, feeling, and planning. In
this chapter, I present a set of problem cases for the orthodox definition. I
then consider three analyses of hope that go beyond the orthodox definition but are nevertheless, I argue, unable to account for the problem cases.
Finally, I present an initial sketch of my analysis, which I call the "incorporation" analysis. I begin with a quick overview of a few core examples of the
orthodox definition.

The Orthodox Definition in the Modern Period

Several philosophers during the seventeenth and eighteenth centuries developed taxonomies of affects, emotions, or passions. Hope appears in many of
these taxonomies, and is usually characterized along lines similar to the orthodox definition. Here are just two examples: Thomas Hobbes and David Hume.

Hobbes classifies hope as a "Pleasure of the Mind," a kind of pleasure
that arises from the thought of possible but not present pleasant outcomes.
There are also "Paynes" of the mind, arising from the thought of possible
but not present unpleasant outcomes. Hobbes sometimes treats these Pleasures and Paynes as distinct categories, but also sometimes includes the pains
under the heading "Pleasures" of the mind, much in the way contemporary

philosophers often treat aversion as a kind of desire. In the latter mode, Hobbes identifies seven simple Pleasures of the Mind, which he also calls simple "Passions": "Appetite, Desire, Love, Aversion, Hate, Joy, and griefe." He builds increasingly complex mental states and processes out of these simple passions. Hope is one of his more basic building blocks:

> "Hope—For Appetite with an opinion of attaining is called HOPE.
> Despaire—The same, without such an opinion, DESPAIRE.
> Feare—Aversion, with an opinion of Hurt from the object, FEARE.
> Courage—The same, with a hope of avoiding that hurt by resistance, COURAGE.
> Anger—Sudden Courage, ANGER.
> Confidence—Constant Hope, CONFIDENCE of ourselves."[1]

... And so on. In Hobbes' view, hope is an important element in other and yet more complex mental states and processes as well, including "Sudden Dejection Weeping"—where a sudden loss of a "vehement hope" causes "Sudden Dejection," a grief due to "opinion of want of power."

According to Hume, hope is one of the "direct" passions. All passions, he believes, are caused by ideas of pleasurable or painful objects, which he also calls "good" and "evil."[2] Direct passions are also directed toward the same objects that cause them. Joy, for example, might be caused by the idea that the working week is over, and will be directed toward, or take as its object, that very same idea. This is by contrast with pride, an indirect passion, caused by the idea of a beautiful home, but directed toward oneself, the owner. So, he writes,

> When good [i.e., pleasure] is certain or probable, it produces JOY. When evil [i.e., pain] is in the same situation there arises GRIEF or SORROW. When either good or evil is uncertain, it gives rise to FEAR or HOPE, according to the degrees of uncertainty on the one side or the other.[3]

Uncertain pleasure or pain gives rise to hope or fear, Hume argues, because one cannot help but vacillate between imagining the pleasure (say) existing and not existing. One therefore also vacillates between feeling joy and sorrow, and these blend to produce hope or fear, depending on which dominates.[4]

---

1 Thomas Hobbes, *Leviathan*, in E. Curley, ed., *Leviathan, with selected variants from the Latin edition of 1668* (Indianapolis: Hackett, 1994 [1651]), par. 14–19.

2 Hume also writes that the direct passions can arise "from a natural impulse or instinct, which is perfectly unaccountable," without requiring even the ideas of pleasure or pain. Examples are bodily appetites and the desires that our loved ones flourish and our enemies be punished. *A Treatise of Human Nature*, L. A. Selby-Bigge, ed., 2nd ed. revised by P. H. Nidditch (Oxford: Clarendon Press, 1975), 2.3.9.

3 Ibid., 2.3.9.

4 Ibid., 2.3.9.

The Orthodox Definition in Recent Philosophy

The orthodox definition crystallizes in work by J. P. Day and R. S. Downie. Day defines hope: "'A hopes that p' is true iff 'A wishes [i.e., desires] that p, and A thinks that p has some degree of probability, however small' is true."[5] And Downie:

> There are two criteria which are independently necessary and jointly sufficient for 'hope that.' The first is that the object of hope must be desired by the hoper. . . . The second . . . is that the object of hope falls within a range of physical possibility which includes the improbable but excludes the certain and the merely logically possible.[6]

Several of the above analyses of hope require some tweaking or clarification. For example, Downie is perhaps not careful enough in his characterization of the second criterion. An outcome need not be possible to be an object of hope—it suffices that the hopeful person believes it is; also, metaphysical possibility is surely sufficient, and physical overly restrictive—a person who believes in miracles can hope for one. Similarly, Hobbes' phrase "opinion of attaining" suggests a degree of uncertainty limited to the upper range of probability judgments. His association of Hope with Confidence also supports this reading. However, the complement of Hope, in the absence of the "opinion of attaining" is Despaire, which for many people does not arise until they are nearly certain the desired outcome is unattainable. It is plausible that Hobbes intended hope to encompass the full range of epistemic uncertainty, from mere possibility to near certainty.

These sorts of refinements aside, the point I wish to highlight is that these advocates of the orthodox definition all presuppose an extremely parsimonious approach to human psychology, whereby there are two basic categories of psychological attitude: motivational and intellective or, as many say today, "conative" and "cognitive." This is the distinction Elizabeth Anscombe famously elucidates in terms of "directions of fit." Some states, the "conative," represent ways the world is *not*, incline the representer to make the world fit them, and persist as long as this fit is missing; other states, the "cognitive," aim to represent the way the world is, and change if the representer discovers they have not achieved this aim.[7]

For many purposes, this may be a useful first cut when carving up the contents of mind. However, the cognitive-conative distinction is broadly recognized as both vague and artful. In the next chapter, I will argue that, for purposes of understanding hope, many related emotional attitudes and,

---

5 J. P. Day, "Hope," *American Philosophical Quarterly* 6.2 (1969): 89.
6 R. S. Downie, "Hope," *Philosophy and Phenomenological Society* 24.2 (1963): 249.
7 G.E.M. Anscombe, *Intention* (Oxford: Basil Blackwell, 1963), section 32.

indeed, human motivation in general, there are better distinctions to rely on, such as that between attitudes beholden to norms of theoretical rationality versus those beholden to exclusively practical norms. There is also an important distinction to draw within the category of motivational states: between motivational states with justificatory or normative content and those without.

The advocates of the orthodox definition, by contrast, either do not recognize the possibility of such alternative distinctions or do not think they are important to an analysis of hope. Not only do they rely on the standard cognitive-conative divide, but they assume hope involves only one kind of motivational state. For example, Hobbes notes that appetite, desire, and love are all the same thing, distinguished only by their objects' existential status: "by desire, we signify the absence of the object; by love, most commonly the presence of the same."[8] These attitudes are all essentially the same because they are all motivational states—for Hobbes, they are literally a form of mechanical motion. Though they are not mechanists, the point also holds for Hume, Day, and Downie; in analyzing hope, they assume it is sufficient to rely on a broad and undifferentiated notion of a motivational state.

Challenge Cases

The inadequacy of the orthodox definition of hope is most salient in relation to a certain set of cases where a person "hopes against hope." There are two crucial features of a hope that is "against hope:" it is hope for an outcome that, first, amounts to overcoming or at least abiding some profound challenge to one's values or welfare; and, second, it is an extremely improbable hope.[9] Hope against hope is a familiar kind of hope—indeed, it is the hope that has drawn the most popular and philosophical attention. It appears, however, that the orthodox definition cannot accommodate the fact that two people with the same powerful desires can, faced with the same slim odds, seemingly differ in their hopes. Consider the following, which is the sort of case that piqued my initial interest in hope:

> *Cancer Research:* Alan and Bess both have advanced, likely terminal cancer, and have exhausted all standard treatment options. They both enroll in an early-phase trial of an experimental drug. They are both informed and understand there is less than 1 percent chance they will receive any medical benefit from their participation in the trial. They have equally

---

8 Hobbes, *Leviathan*, Ch. 6, 3.

9 That is, the hopeful person *believes* the outcome is highly improbable. The reader can assume that, unless I specify otherwise, the probability assignments discussed throughout the book are subjective.

strong desires to find a "miracle cure." Here's how they are different: If asked, Alan will say he does indeed hope the experimental drug will turn out to be, for him at least, a miracle cure. But he will also emphasize how poor a chance 1 percent is, and he rarely appeals to his hope as a justification for his decisions, moods, or feelings. For example, he says he was motivated to enroll in the trial primarily by a desire to benefit future people with cancer. Bess, instead, while noting that it is almost certain she will not be cured by the experimental drug, says the bare possibility is what keeps her going, and often appeals to her hope as a justification for her decisions, moods, and feelings. One percent is enough, she says. She hopes to be the 1 percent, and that is her main reason for enrolling in the trial. Both people hope for a cure, but Bess is the person we would describe as "hoping against hope"; there is some sense in which her hope is higher or greater or stronger than Alan's.

The way cases like this challenge the orthodox definition is fairly obvious: Alan and Bess don't differ in their desires or in the probability they assign to a cure, but their hopes do differ—so it seems that the orthodox definition must leave something out.

Ariel Meirav points to a related set of challenge cases for the orthodox definition.[10] These are cases where this definition is unable to distinguish hope from despair. I will call Meirav's two cases *Shawshank Redemption* and *Lottery Ticket*. *Shawshank Redemption* comes from Stephen King's story, "Rita Hayworth and the Shawshank Redemption," and the movie based on it.[11] Andy and Red are both serving life sentences in prison. They both desperately want to be free, and they both believe there is some miniscule chance they might succeed in escaping. Yet Andy holds out hope for an escape and a life of freedom, while Red only despairs:

> Andy lives in the hope of escape, whereas Red despairs of this. Indeed, Red thinks that hope should be resisted, suppressed, for hoping in this virtually hopeless situation would threaten his sanity . . . Red will say, "I grant you it is *possible*, but the chance is only one in a thousand!" whereas Andy will say, "I grant you the chance is only one in a thousand, but it is *possible!*"[12]

Meirav pushes this case against the orthodox definition (which he calls the "Standard Definition"), along with two alternative proposals from Luc Bovens and Philip Pettit. We will come to these alternatives shortly; for the moment, I bring up the case as a challenge to the orthodox definition. Red and Andy

---

10 Meirav, "The Nature of Hope."
11 Steven King, "Rita Hayworth and the Shawshank Redemption," *Different Seasons* (New York, NY: Signet, 1982).
12 Meirav, "The Nature of Hope," 222–23.

plausibly share the same desire and probability estimates, but their attitudes are deeply opposed, so it seems this definition has left something out.

Lottery Ticket makes a similar point: Meirav brings home a lottery ticket; he and his wife have equally strong desires to win and agree about the extremely low probability of this outcome. But Meirav hopes to win and his wife does not. Although Meirav describes the inadequacy of the theories he attacks as a failure to distinguish hope and despair, there is no mention of despair in *Lottery Ticket*. This, I take it, does not really detract from the argument—this case, just like cases of hoping against hope, highlights the fact that, in the face of very slim odds, some people are more hopeful than others, even when there are no differences in desire or probability estimates between the two groups. In what follows, I focus on *Cancer Research* and *Shawshank Redemption*, assuming the reader can see how the arguments extend to *Lottery Ticket*.

The proponent of the orthodox definition could try to accommodate these cases by arguing either that Bess's and Andy's *desires* are actually stronger than are Alan's and Red's, or that Bess and Andy actually *believe the odds are better* than do Alan and Red. Consider the first response, in terms of "actual" desires. One might argue that Bess's stronger desire is evidenced or even defined by the fact that she is willing to do more in pursuit of a cure. No doubt there is some version of Alan and Bess that this argument accurately describes. However, there is no reason to think the case as originally described must be mistaken. Consider this, as well: for anyone who has had to make a weighty medical or other personal decision on the basis of a probability judgment, it is a familiar experience that the same probability can look good some days, and bad others. From week to week, or even day to day, one may be more and less motivated to pursue an outcome with a 20 percent probability. And it certainly doesn't ring true to the experience of such fluctuation to insist that the strength of one's desire is what is fluctuating.[13]

There are two problems with the second line of response. First, all parties may show all signs of assigning the same probability—avowing it to be *n*, being willing to bet at the same odds, selecting *n* cards out of a hundred to provide a visual representation of the chances, and so on. It strains credulity to insist that, in spite of all this, one party must implicitly believe the chances are better than does the other. Second, this response may run into some normative trouble. Many people have a strong intuition that Bess's hope is no less *rational* than Alan's, and that Andy is no less rational than

---

13 I should note that there is a certain sense in which I think these characters do differ in their "desires." I will argue that all of them find the relevant outcomes equally *attractive* or *compelling*, but that Bess and Andy incorporate their attractions into their agency by treating them as practical reasons, in a way that Alan and Red refuse to do. As mentioned above, however, the proponents of the orthodox definition all treat "desire" as an undifferentiated category, and so cannot accommodate this distinction.

Red (as long as Bess and Andy aren't doing wildly imprudent things on the basis of their hopes). Assuming probability assignments are beholden to an evidential norm and the parties in each of the cases have the same evidential basis for their probability assignments, however, it appears the orthodox definition cannot mesh with this intuition. The next chapter will present an argument for holding subjective probability estimates to an evidential norm. For now, I just want to note the problem such a norm poses for the orthodox definition. The proponent of the orthodox definition should not attempt to accommodate these cases by arguing that the person who seems more hopeful implicitly believes the chances are better than the subjectively available evidence establishes; the evidentialist norm would entail that this person's hope is irrational. And while we certainly shouldn't assume such hopes are necessarily rational, nor should we leap so quickly to their irrationality, simply in the interest of preserving this definition.

Thus, the orthodox definition appears inadequate to account for an important set of cases that are pre-theoretically *paradigmatic* examples of hope.[14] To be clear, my claim here is not that these cases represent a special form of hope to which the orthodox definition is inadequate, but rather that the orthodox definition is inadequate to all forms of hope; cases of hoping against hope are simply those where this inadequacy is most salient. I will return to this point at the end of chapter 2. I turn now to three extant alternative analyses of hope. These alternatives, from Luc Bovens, Ariel Meirav, and Philip Pettit, are all on the right track, each in its own way. In the end, however, each is unable to both plausibly capture the appearance of hope and account for the challenge cases.

First Analysis: Luc Bovens and Mental Imaging

Bovens argues that hope entails what he calls "mental imaging." This is supposed to be a condition that goes beyond the orthodox definition, but I think he has simply zeroed in on one important element of desire. Here is the core of Bovens' argument:

> Sophie shows up late at some party and asks me very self-confidently whether I had been hoping she would come. Now suppose that I did indeed believe that Sophie might come and that I consider her to be a welcome guest—i.e., I prefer her coming to the party to her not coming to the party. Still, it seems to me that it would be a lie to say that I had been hoping she would come, unless I had devoted at least some mental energy

---

14 When I say these cases are "paradigmatic" instances of hope, I do not mean that they are the most common kind of hope, but rather that they are *exemplars* of hope in its fullest sense. They are the kinds of cases where the nature of the phenomenon is most salient.

to the question whether she would or would not come to the party—e.g., I had been looking at the clock wondering whether Sophie would come, I had been turning my head earlier to check whether Sophie was amongst some newly arrived guests, etc. Let us name this devotion of mental energy to what it would be like if some projected state of the world were to materialize "mental imaging."[15]

Bovens believes mental imaging is a necessary condition for hope. He is, I believe, correct that hope entails at least the disposition to entertain certain kinds of thoughts about the hoped-for outcome, but he is incorrect in thinking that this is the key to the orthodox definition's inadequacy.

According to the most widely accepted philosophical conception of desire, it is a set of dispositions: a disposition to try to bring about the hoped-for outcome, a disposition to feel pleasure in anticipating that outcome, a disposition to attend to the outcome's desirable features and to possible routes to it, a disposition to think about the outcome and imagine what it would be like for it to happen, and so on.[16] Suppose that, in telling the story about Sophie, Bovens had specified some of these dispositions. It's not clear whether introducing these dispositions would go beyond the original descriptions of the desire for Sophie to attend, "I consider her to be a welcome guest" and "I prefer her coming to the party to her not coming to the party," but in the absence of any such dispositions it would be strange to attribute even the desire to the narrator. Suppose further that these dispositions did not manifest at any point before Sophie's arrival—more people arrived than he had expected, and he was too busy setting out the chips and dips, introducing people, and running out for ice to think about much else. Nevertheless, it is true that, if he had had the time to spare for thoughts about who specifically had arrived, he would have thought how nice it would be if Sophie showed up. If all this were true, then it would be strange to say that he did not hope Sophie would come to the party, even though this hope was latent.[17]

Granted, it might still seem disingenuous to answer Sophie's coy question affirmatively, but that is because she is really asking whether he was *thinking about her*. Observe that, if Sophie had asked, "Did you *want* me to come?" rather than "Were you hoping I would come?" an enthusiastic affirmative answer would also seem disingenuous: "Sure, Sophie, I hadn't had time to

---

15   Luc Bovens, "The Value of Hope," 674.

16   Philip Pettit and Michael Smith, "Backgrounding Desire," *Philosophical Review* 99 (1990): 565–92.

17   In fact, there is something missing from this description of the narrator's hope: the incorporation element I will come to later in this chapter—the point here is that it is not Bovens' "mental imaging" that is missing.

notice you weren't here, but I wanted you to come!" Thus I conclude that, while it may be true that mental imaging is an important element of hope, this alone does not render the orthodox definition inadequate.

Moreover, adding mental imaging to the orthodox definition does not help us with the challenge cases. Alan and Bess could spend equal amounts of time thinking about a cure, and they might even have the exact same mental images, while still exhibiting the differences that lead us to attribute a stronger or greater hope to Bess. And Red and Andy could both dream about life outside of prison, while continuing to despair and hope, respectively. So Bovens' addition to the orthodox definition doesn't compensate for its inadequacy. Nevertheless, he is surely right that an important element of hope is the way it engages our attention and imagination.[18]

Second Analysis: Ariel Meirav and External Factors

Meirav focuses our attention on the fact that hoping for an outcome entails acknowledging that whether the outcome obtains depends at least in part on "external factors"—that is, agents and events beyond one's control. He proposes that what makes the difference between hoping and despairing in cases like *Shawshank Redemption* is the attitude one takes toward one or some of these external factors:

> [I]n a wide range of types of cases desire and probability assignment do not in themselves determine whether one hopes for or despairs of a prospect. What does determine this (in combination with desire and probability assignment) is one's attitude to a relevant external factor: If one views the external factor as good, then one hopes for the prospect. If one views it as not good, then one despairs of it.[19]

According to Meirav, to see an external factor as "good" is to see it as operating in your interest, so that it will cooperate in the realization of your hope, unless there is a good reason—a reason you would accept—for it not to.

Note one tricky thing about the External Factor analysis: believing an external factor operates on one's behalf can raise the probability one assigns to the hoped-for outcome. However, if that is what is going on in these cases, the orthodox definition is a sufficient analysis of them. So Meirav must stipulate that, while Andy views some external factor as working in favor of his escape, he does not thereby think his escape is more likely than Red does.

18 Drawing on Dewey, pragmatist philosopher Patrick Shade also gives imagination a central role in hope. See Shade, *Habits of Hope: A Pragmatic Theory* (Nashville, TN: Vanderbilt University Press, 2001), esp. chapter 1.

19 Meirav, "The Nature of Hope," 230.

Even with this stipulation in place, Meirav's analysis is ultimately unsuccessful. For one thing, it excludes certain genuine cases of hope. Specifically, it precludes hoping for an outcome that one believes depends on arbitrary or unjust factors. I cannot, for example, hope for a political outcome resulting from a flawed political process. If I see this process as unlikely to operate in a reasonable manner, then I cannot see it as "good" in Meirav's sense, and so I cannot hope it will produce the outcome I desire. (Assume, too, that I do not believe in fortune or fate, so Meirav cannot respond that I must believe one of these operates in my favor.)

More important than this problem, however, is that the external factor analysis cannot do the work Meirav sets it. Surely Andy and Red could both see the crucial external factor as good and yet still hope and despair, respectively. Suppose they both believe this factor is one of the prison guards. They could both view the guard as wanting to help them escape, and take it he will do so unless there is a good reason not to, and yet still differ in the way originally described. This is particularly clear if we specify that they both believe it is extremely unlikely the warden will have the opportunity to help them. They can see him as working in their favor, but still express the same hopeful and despairing attitudes: "I grant you the chance is one in a thousand, but it is *possible!*" versus "I grant it is *possible*, but the chance is only *one in a thousand!*" Similarly, I see no reason to think the cancer research participants, Alan and Bess, must differ in their assessments of some external factor to exhibit the differences they do.

Bovens observes that the hopeful person tends to engage in certain mental activities; but I argued that this fact alone does not distinguish the more hopeful from the less, or the hopeful from the despairing. The point we should take from Meirav is that the hopeful person sees those mental activities *as justified*, while the person who despairs sees them as *unjustified*. That is, while Meirav is wrong about what "factor" the hopeful person's justification appeals to, he is right that the difference between hope and despair is a matter of the justificatory attitude one adopts. He is also right to call this attitude a way of "seeing" rather than a belief. Philip Pettit's analysis, too, makes use of these observations.

Third Analysis: Philip Pettit and Cognitive Resolve

Pettit believes the orthodox definition is an accurate analysis of a "lowest common denominator" or "superficial" sense of hope. However, he thinks this view fails to capture what is interesting about certain central cases of hope and that, in particular, it does not give any insight into why we value hope in dire circumstances. He proposes that "substantial" hope involves, in addition to desire and a subjective probability estimate, a "cognitive resolve" to "act as if [the hoped-for] prospect were going to obtain or as if there were a good chance that it was going to obtain."[20]

He develops this proposal in parallel with an account of precaution. In the case of precaution, he writes, one sets one's beliefs about the actually probability of an *un*desired outcome "off-line":

> [Y]ou are not the slave of the beliefs that are immediately relevant to a decision. . . . You are capable of placing yourself at a distance from them and putting yourself under the control of an assumption you may not strictly endorse. You can assume the profile of someone you are not: someone with the cautious belief that the cost will be [more than you in fact estimate it will be].[21]

Hope is essentially the reverse of precaution:

> When hope of any kind is present, however superficial, then there is a prospect that the agent believes may or may not obtain, but unlike the prospect for which precaution is fitted, this is something that the agent desires to obtain. Hope would take a parallel form to precaution, then, if there were any reason in such a case why the agent should be moved to act as if that desired prospect were going to obtain or as if there were a good chance that it was going to obtain.[22]

Pettit's analysis definitely gets something right with regard to our challenge cases. Andy has decided to act as if he is going to escape.[23] He has actually set up a way to access his money and get himself to Mexico, in the event he is able to escape from prison. Red, of course, has made no plans for a life of freedom. Similarly, Alan is unlikely to plan for much that depends on the experimental drug turning out to be a miracle cure, while Bess may very well make plans contingent on living well past her expected lifespan. These kinds of choices, this *reliance* on a hoped-for outcome, are as much marks of hope as are the mental imaging identified by Bovens.

However, there is an important qualification to make here. It seems unlikely that either Andy or Bess would act and speak as they do if they had adopted Pettit's cognitive resolve under the current characterization. The cases change, if we try to read them in Pettit's terms. Andy would no longer say, "I grant you the chance is only one in a thousand, but it is *possible!*" Instead, he would say something like "I grant you the chance is only one in a

---

20 Pettit, "Hope and Its Place in Mind," 157.

21 Ibid., 155.

22 Ibid., 157.

23 Meirav argues that Red, too, could adopt this resolve, while continuing to despair—he might, for example, adopt this resolve only to placate Andy. The problem with Meirav's argument is that Pettit specifies that the hopeful person resolves to act as she does *in order to fend off despair or emotional vicissitudes.* If Red did that, it is not clear he could continue to despair.

thousand, but don't think about *that!*" Cognitive resolve, understood as the resolution to act as if the hoped-for outcome *has a good chance of occurring*, does not look much like hope. This is even clearer if we imagine Bess acting with the kind of cognitive resolve Pettit describes. Her behavior would not, I think, resemble the behavior of the people we are apt to describe as hoping against hope, in such circumstances. If she truly acted as if there were a good chance she would receive the "miracle cure," then she would not do significant planning for the likely event that her cancer kills her in the near future (which *ex hypothesi* she assigns a high probability, even though she has set the assignment off-line). That is, Pettit's analysis of hope puts it in tension with taking precautionary steps against the event that the hoped-for outcome does not obtain. But the trope in these situations is "hope for the best, plan for the worst"—precaution is a natural companion of hope. People in such situations often extensively prepare for their deaths, drawing up wills, resolving conflicts with loved ones, doing the things they always wanted to do, and so on. But they do not hope any the less for undertaking these activities.

It seems to me Pettit has described something more like faith than hope. A person who has faith in a Christian God who will reward virtue and punish vice acts as if this is true, taking no precautionary steps against the possibility that she is wrong. She does not worship other gods or occasionally partake in worldly pleasure rather than satisfy her religious duties—more specifically, she does not do these things *just in case* the other religions or the atheists turn out to be right. Or, to take a secular case, when I *have faith* in you, this is different than my *hoping that* you will be reliable, and the difference is largely that, in the case of hope but not faith, I may carry mad money.[24]

The point is that, while the person who hopes often relies on the hoped-for outcome in making her plan, she also typically has a *back-up plan*. For example, while Andy does set up his funds for the event he escapes, he has also done his best to ensure that, if he is unable to escape, no one else will be able to access his hidden money. This is what I will call "hedged reliance." Similarly, if Bess makes plans contingent on a miracle cure, she is likely to form back-up plans. So, for example, if she buys tickets for a cruise next year, she will make sure they can be transferred to someone else.

Perhaps Pettit merely states his position too strongly. Perhaps we should say hope involves acting as if the hoped-for outcome is *more likely* than one actually believes it is, while allowing for significant uncertainty and, thereby, precaution. This is a fairly minor modification of his position, as he originally states it. According to this modified version of Pettit's account, the research participant who hopes against hope relies on something like the following rationale, articulate or not: *I know the truth is that I almost certainly won't*

---

24   I will discuss faith and its relation to hope at length in chapter 4.

be cured by this drug, but that truth is too crushing; if I focus on it, I will live out my few remaining days in misery. Instead, then, I will go forward as if that miracle cure has a better chance of happening—I should prepare for the event that it doesn't, but I will also see extended life as a real possibility.

Again, though, this just doesn't ring true to the way many such people talk about their experience.[25] They're more likely to say something like this: *I know the truth is that I almost certainly won't be cured by this drug . . . but, you know what? A tiny chance is better than no chance! That 1 percent is my lifeline, and I'm going to hang onto it.* "I will be the 1 percent" is a refrain familiar to anyone who spends time around early-phase cancer research participants. And it is entirely reasonable to describe this person, too, as hoping against hope, even while she bases her plans and actions on her belief that the chances of a miracle cure are miniscule.

One might object that this is only an apparent counterexample, that the person who vows she will "be the 1 percent" is essentially resolving to treat 1 percent like a higher probability than it actually is. If so, hope does seem to involve, contrary to Pettit's claims, some self-deception. Besides, I don't think this is the right way to interpret this way of hoping against hope. The person who takes 1 percent as a reasonable basis for hoping against hope doesn't thereby think of 1 percent as 25 percent, or anything like that—she simply sees 1 percent as enough to go forward. Consider the way the same odds can seem high or low depending on whether they apply to a feared or a hoped-for outcome: 17 percent strikes many as a scary prospect when it refers to the chance of failed remission, while it strikes many as an excellent prospect when it refers to the chance of going into remission. These shifts are not shifts in a person's assessment of the odds; they are rather a sort of Gestalt shift on the very same odds. We are capable of evaluating the odds as better or worse, depending in part on whether we are considering an undesirable or desirable outcome. Similarly, different people may evaluate the same odds differently, even when those odds apply to equally desired outcomes.

In other words, while Pettit is right that hoping means being disposed to act as if the hoped-for outcome is going to occur, or is likely to occur, he is wrong about the hopeful person's *rationale* for acting in this way. The hopeful person doesn't act like this because she has decided to act as if the outcome is indeed more likely to occur than she believes it is; rather, she acts like this because she sees the outcome's probability as good enough to permit it. She doesn't say to herself, "set that miniscule probability off-line;" she says, "focus on the fact that even a miniscule probability is a *possibility*."

---

25 Moreover, as Chris Melenovsky pointed out to me, it is possible to go through the cognitive resolve process but not hope at all. One merely recognizes the pragmatic benefits of acting as if something were the case.

Final Analysis: Incorporation

Drawing on both the strengths and shortcomings of each of the above three analyses, we can see that the key difference between the characters in the challenge cases is that the hopeful people stand ready to *justify* dedicating certain kinds of attention and thought to the outcome, as well as hedged reliance on the outcome in their plans; moreover, they stand ready to appeal to the outcome's probability as part of their justification for these activities.

I dedicate the rest of this chapter and the next to developing these observations into a full analysis of hope. First, we need to be clear on what these "certain kinds of attention and thought" are. For even a person who despairs of an outcome may dedicate a good deal of attention and thought to it, and may appeal to the outcome's probability in his justification. Putting the difference vaguely, for the moment, it is that the hopeful person sees *positive* attention and thought as justified, while the despairing person sees only *negative* attention and thought as justified.[26] This difference in valence is a matter not of the *content* of the attention and thought, but rather of the accompanying *feeling*. That is, the hopeful person sees it as justified not only to dedicate attention and thought to the hoped-for outcome, but also to experience a certain positive feeling or emotion I will call "hopeful anticipation" (or just "anticipation") while doing so.[27]

Second, we need to be clear about the exact attitude the hopeful person takes toward the probability she assigns the hoped-for outcome. Both Meirav and Pettit treat hope as different from belief, and they are right to do so. Meirav does so only implicitly, by his use of "seeing as" language. Pettit explicitly argues that hopefully acting as if an outcome is likely to occur is *pragmatically* rational: it is justified if it prevents one from succumbing to despair in the face of the true odds, and also allows one to pursue a steady course of action without constantly readjusting in response to fluctuating evidence regarding the outcome's probability. In the cases where hope arises, the *belief*

---

26 Are negative feelings not involved in hope sometimes, such as the fear of disappointment? I am inclined to say that, strictly speaking, negative feelings—particularly endorsed ones of the sort I am discussing—are manifestations of different attitudes (such as the fear of disappointment). This is not to say that anticipation is always entirely *pleasant*—it can manifest as a kind of heart-pounding breathlessness that verges on the painful. Also, phenomenologically speaking, it can be quite difficult to disentangle attitudes that go so naturally together, such as the hope for success and the fear of failure.

27 In general, I am going to avoid the term "emotion" throughout this book. This is because I do not subscribe to any particular "theory of the emotions"—the things we call emotions vary too widely, in my view, to be caught up by a single theory. In particular, there are some things, like hope and love and normative expectation, that are in part dispositions to think it justified to feel certain other things, like anticipation and concern and resentment. Yet it is not a far fetch to call some or all of these things "emotions."

that the hoped-for outcome is likely to obtain would violate an evidential-ist norm and, therefore, be epistemically irrational. The cognitive resolve of hope is not beholden to this norm, however, and so is not epistemically irra-tional, either.[28] Neither Pettit nor Meirav, however, attempts to articulate the nature of "acting as if" or "seeing as," or to argue that they are not beholden to the same rational norms as belief. In the next chapter, I explain what it is to "see" a probability in a hopeful way, and provide an argument for holding this attitude to purely instrumental norms of rationality.

Finally, we need to be clear about what it means to "stand ready to justify" hopeful activities and feelings. I argue in the next chapter that humans are ca-pable of two distinct though interacting modes of motivation. One relies on a representation without justificatory content—this is how most Humeans or even merely Humean-influenced philosophers think of the attitude they call "desire," but I will eventually call this attitude "being attracted to" or "com-pelled by" an outcome, in order to more clearly distinguish it from more ra-tionalist conceptions of desire. The other crucial mode of human motivation relies on representing considerations as justificatory reasons for practical ac-tivity. When we hope, we deploy both kinds of representation: we *incorporate* our attraction to an uncertain outcome into our agency by treating it as a reason for hopeful activities and feelings.

A note on the term "incorporate." I take it, of course, from Henry Allison, who argues that Kant's action theory relies on the "Incorporation Thesis," according to which an inclination cannot move us to act without first being incorporated into a maxim.[29] There is thus a fair amount of technical vo-cabulary in the room when I talk about "incorporation." However, the idea I am aiming to capture is fairly simple: it is that we are capable of reflecting on our own attitudes and endorsing or rejecting them as reasons for action. When we do endorse, say, a desire ("attraction") as a reason for action—that is, in order to justify our action we appeal in part to the desire—we thereby "incorporate" it into our rational agency, our ability to act for reasons. I will say a good deal more on this subject in the next chapter.

Hopeful Thoughts: Fantasy

As I argued above, the activities Bovens labels "mental imaging"—that is, paying attention to an outcome or the circumstances that would lead to it, imagining what it would be like if it occurred, and so on—are not specific to

---

28 Pettit does not put the point in terms of the applicability of an evidentialist norm, but he does argue that hope can be rational because it does not involve believing false propositions or deceiving oneself about the true probabilities.

29 Henry Allison, *Kant's Theory of Freedom* (New York: Cambridge University Press, 1990), 5–6.

hope; they are manifestations of *desire*.[30] What is specific to hope is standing ready to justify these activities in a particular way. Since hoping involves endorsing certain manifestations of desire, it is worth going into some detail about what these manifestations are like. Here, I focus on an activity I call "fantasizing" about what it would be like for the outcome to occur. Later, in chapter 3, understanding this activity and how it can influence deliberation will prove crucial to specifying the circumstances in which hope has a special sustaining power.

Fantasizing is not necessarily related to the "phantasies" of Freudian or object relations psychoanalytic theory.[31] If one of these theories is correct, perhaps fantasizing is explained in terms of phantasies, but the activity is identifiable without appeal to these theories. Fantasies have two crucial features. First, they have narrative structure. They are in this way different from other kinds of imaginative activities—such as picturing a spot or mentally constructing a chimera—whose objects are atemporal. For example, a person who desires to win an award may fantasize about the award ceremony: the room is set up with tables and full of people; she feels anticipation or anxiety; the presenter speaks on other matters until tension is high, then dramatically pauses before announcing her name; she is elated, trying not to cry. And so on. Fantasies tell stories. These stories may be realistic or not—fantasies need not be *fantastical*.

Second, fantasizing has an egoistic function. That is, fantasizing is a way of imagining some of one's desires satisfied. I take it this is something like what Freud is getting at when he says phantasizing is about "wish-fulfillment," but we still need not bring the apparatus of psychoanalytic theory on board to comprehend the notion of a fantasy. The point is a conceptual one: we need to connect fantasizing with imaginary desire-satisfaction in order to distinguish fantasies from similar but distinct narrative imaginative exercises.

In particular, we need to recognize the egoistic function of fantasizing in order to distinguish it from both recalling and composing narratives. It is tempting to base these distinctions on perspective, and claim fantasies are necessarily first-personal, while one can recall or compose a scene from a third-person perspective. It is true that, in a great many fantasies, the fantasizer takes the part of one of the characters—either giving herself a role, or taking the part of another real or fictional person—and "experiences" the

---

30 My arguments here are relevant to both those who hold rationalist conceptions of desire and those who share the anti-rationalist view I develop in the next chapter, so I do not make the distinction here, or advert to "attractions" rather than "desires".

31 Sigmund Freud, *The Interpretation of Dreams*, [1911], 3rd ed., A. A. Brill, trans.: http://psywww.com/books/interp/toc.htm. Melanie Klein, *The Selected Melanie Klein* (New York: Free Press, 1987). See also Richard Wollheim, *The Thread of Life* (Cambridge, MA: Harvard University Press, 1984), for a compelling discussion of phantasy and philosophy of mind informed by object relations theory.

events unfolding from a first-person perspective. This is not an essential feature of fantasies, however. The person wanting to win the award may fantasize about the judges' cloistered deliberations, and I, a friend of this person, may fantasize about the ceremony, without including myself among the attendees. So there isn't a formal constraint on the perspective taken by the fantasizer.

Indeed, it is possible to recall, compose, and fantasize via exactly the same narrative, and from exactly the same point of view. One fantasizes about being Harry Potter, seeing the train to Hogwarts for the first time, and one follows Rowling's written scene to the letter, but still there is something about this activity that makes it fantasizing and not simply (re)calling the scene to mind. Additionally, it is not the fact that the scene isn't original to the fantasizer that makes it different from Rowling's activity, supposing she imagined the scene in her head before she wrote it down, even if she imagined it from Harry's point of view. This isn't to claim that novels are never the product of fantasizing, or that the Harry Potter series isn't in part the product of Rowling's fantasies. However, we all recognize that there is a difference between mental composition and fantasizing. The difference is that the fantasizer imagines being Harry as a way of enjoying the imaginary satisfaction of one of her desires—perhaps to be special, to be rescued, to be released from the constraints of everyday life, or simply to be amazed.

Some of our fantasies are perverse or disturbing to us, or are about events we would never want to occur. Nevertheless, in calling an imaginary narrative exercise "fantasizing," we are *inter alia* indicating its egoistic function. If we believed that it truly didn't serve this function, we would not call it that. Consider a neighbor who "fantasizes" that a recent rash of robberies in one's idyllic town was committed by "a group of Mexicans in a van." The point of calling this a fantasy is to indicate that the neighbor's theory is more sinister than paranoia—it is a way of confirming her prejudices. When she imagines the van of Mexicans prowling the night streets, it provides imaginary satisfaction of her desire to be right about Mexicans, or to be morally superior to Mexicans.[32]

Fantasy serves an egoistic function, and hope is grounded in desire. That is why, for so many people, hope is commonly associated with dreams and imagination. Other mental activities lack the connection to desire, and may instead be manifestations of fear or other aversive attitudes. Consider another case from Bovens: a person attends car races, believes an accident is possible, desires to see one, and spends time imagining one.[33] Bovens argues that, in this case, we have all of the necessary and sufficient conditions for hope, unlike in a case where a racing enthusiast realizes that he has been attending the most dangerous races and placing himself in the best spots to see an accident,

32 Thanks to Valerie Martin for the example and discussion of fantasizing's egoistic function.
33 Bovens, "The Value of Hope," 679.

but has never thought about an accident. I would argue, contra Bovens, that the desire to see an accident implies at least the disposition to spend time imagining one, and that the two cases are not conceptually distinct. However, the point I want to draw from the case where the enthusiast does imagine an accident is different: there are narrative imaginings that are manifestations of desire and there are others that are manifestations of aversion.

Suppose the racing enthusiast has a strong aversion to an accident occurring, but he also has a seditious desire to see one. He may manifest either the aversion or the desire by imagining what it would be like to see an accident, tell his friends about it, and so on. There isn't a ready label for the kind of imaginative activity that manifests aversion, but there is such an activity. We engage in it, for example, in order to prepare ourselves for bad news or unpleasant experiences. Alternatively, his imaginings may be fantasies about the accident, manifesting his seditious desire in spite of his strong aversion. The third possibility is the simplest and, I take it, the one Bovens had in mind: he has a desire for and no aversion to the accident, and fantasizes about one happening. There is a fourth possibility that arises because of the wonderful and troubling capacity of the human psyche to be deeply conflicted. This possibility is, of course, that Bovens' character not only both desires and has an aversion to an accident, but also engages in imaginative activities that manifest both states. It's easy enough to see how sometimes he might imagine the accident in order to enjoy imaginary desire-satisfaction, while at other times he might instead imagine it in connection with an aversion, perhaps to make it easier to cope with the event if it someday occurs. We should also, however, leave open the possibility that the same imagined narrative could serve both purposes at once—it would thus be both fantasizing and whatever this other kind of activity is. An imaginative activity that had both egoistic and bracing functions would be, among other things, an important tool for preparing oneself for the satisfaction of desires one repudiates.

I am not claiming the mental activities that the hopeful person stands ready to justify are limited to fantasizing. Some people are not prone to constructing narratives, and their hopes may manifest instead in, for example, prayer or its secular cousin, pleading with the universe ("*Please* let the news be good!"); other people's hopes may manifest primarily through a feeling of anticipation and hedged reliance. However, I do believe fantasizing is a common manifestation of hope.[34] So this will be one of the paradigmatic hopeful activities I focus on in the rest of this book.

Now, since fantasizing is a manifestation of desire, it is also a paradigmatic despairing activity. Some people who despair of a desired outcome,

---

34 In November 2008, I surveyed sixty-seven undergraduates on their hopes regarding the outcome of the U.S. presidential election. The most common reported manifestation of hope regarding the outcome was "imagining my candidate winning."

like Red from *Shawshank Redemption*, see the outcome's probability as making it illegitimate and unjustifiable to dedicate *any* thought whatsoever to the outcome—fantasizing about life outside of prison is a waste of time and only makes him feel worse, so he does his best to refrain from it. Some people who despair, however, wallow in fantasies about the practically unattainable outcome and see this as justifiable. Their justification relies on attaching such value to the desired outcome that life is essentially meaningless without it—it is not a waste of time to think on it despairingly, because there is no better use of their time; and terrible is exactly how they believe they ought to feel. This is the sense of "despair" that is perhaps most paradigmatic: although we talk of "despairing" of various outcomes, we usually get on with our lives. The real despair that overwhelms, paralyzes, agonizes, is the despair that occupies one's mind.[35]

Hope and despair are complements, or contrast attitudes.[36] The above observations about despair thus indicate there is more to hope than seeing an activity such as fantasizing about a hoped-for outcome as justified: the hopeful person also sees it as justifiable to *feel good* as a result of her fantasies. There is, in fact, a specific feeling that manifests hope. This feeling is best specified through a comparison with an attitude closely related to hope: positive expectation.

Hopeful Feelings: Anticipation

Cognitive scientists Maria Miceli and Cristiano Castelfranchi have published a number of papers on anticipatory states like anxiety, expectation, and hope. Their analysis of hope is a version of the orthodox definition. Hope, in their view, has two "basic ingredients:" a "goal or wish: that the hoped-for outcome occurs" and a "mere belief of *possibility* about [the outcome]." [37] This latter condition, they emphasize, distinguishes hope from what they call "positive expectation" (in an earlier paper, they used the term "hopecast" instead of "positive expectation"[38]). A positive expectation of an outcome is a desire for the outcome plus a "forecast" or "prediction" that it will occur, where a forecast is the assignment of a probability equal to or greater than an even chance. In other words, they want to reserve the term "possibility"

---

35 In chapter 4, I will identify a more specific form of overwhelming despair, which is the despair whereby one embraces one's own destruction, i.e., "existential" despair.

36 *Pace* Anthony J. Steinbock, "The Phenomenology of Despair," *International Journal of Philosophical Studies* 15.3 (2007): 435–51.

37 Maria Miceli and Cristiano Castelfranchi, "Hope: The Power of Wish and Possibility," *Theory and Psychology* 20.2 (2010): 257.

38 Maria Miceli and Cristiano Castelfranchi, "The Mind and the Future: The (Negative) Power of Expectations," *Theory and Psychology* 12 (2002): 335–66.

for probabilities less than 0.5, and "probability" for anything above; and they claim hope involves believing an outcome is "possible," while expectation involves believing it is "probable." They grant that "hope" in a broad sense encompasses positive expectations, but suggest it is methodologically valuable to distinguish the two along the lines they lay out. They defend the distinction by appealing to ordinary language, whereby it is common to contrast hope and expectation: "For instance, Mary can say 'I don't expect that he will come, I *just* hope so.'"[39]

Now, it is certainly true that we sometimes mark a distinction between hope and expectation, and that we appear to do so on the basis of how likely we believe the outcome is. We also do tend to mark a distinction between possibility and probability on a similar basis—"Well, it's not *probable*," we might say of some unlikely outcome, "but it is *possible*." However, the selection of an even chance as the boundary seems arbitrary, especially when it comes to the distinction between hope and expectation. Indeed, any attempt to distinguish hope and expectation in terms of a specific and fixed probability assignment alone— 0.7? 0.88?—is arbitrary. Surely this boundary varies from group to group, individual to individual, and even from context to context for the same individual. For example, if the stakes resting on a desired outcome are extremely high, it may be more difficult for an individual to cross from hope to expectation. This variation is because the difference between hope and expectation is a matter of how one *sees* a probability, and not the probability alone.

I should say this is the difference between hope and expectation, *insofar as there is one*. I share Miceli's and Castelfranchi's linguistic intuition: it strikes me that it rarely makes sense to speak of hoping for and expecting the same outcome. When people say they "hope and expect" I will do something, it rubs me the wrong way, because it seems to me they are both trying to exert a kind of pressure, by expressing expectation, and pretending they are not, by expressing hope. However, I gather from conversations that others do not share this intuition—they think hope and expectation are perfectly compatible. I think I can explain these diverging intuitions in what follows. The basic idea is that the feelings typical of hope and expectation are distinguishable members of a class or family, and our talk about the two attitudes can focus on either the distinguishing features or the shared membership.

Based on the distinction they draw between hope and expectation, Miceli and Castelfranchi infer a number of affective patterns associated with the two attitudes. I think their mistake lies in trying to give a definition of hope independent of these patterns—instead, the disposition to display the sorts of patterns they identify is itself a constitutive element of the difference between hope and expectation.

---

39   Miceli, "Hope: The Power of Wish and Possibility," 257.

The focus here is on our likely affective responses to the disappointment and fulfillment of hopes and expectations. Expectation brings with it a sense of quasi-entitlement that hope lacks, with the result that disappointed expectations produce greater anger than disappointed hopes. Although Miceli and Castelfranchi do not explicitly refer to the philosophical concept of the *reactive attitudes*, the anger they discuss in association with frustrated expectation is closely akin to these attitudes, especially personal anger and resentment. These are attitudes we feel when we hold people responsible for their behavior. As P. F. Strawson argues, part of what it is to see oneself or another as a responsible and free agent is to stand poised to respond to indecent behavior with feelings of guilt (regarding one's own behavior) or resentment (regarding another's).[40] Positive expectations with regard to non-agential events carry with them only analogues of the reactive attitudes; we do not (often) hold the non-agential world responsible for the events that take place within it. We do, however, respond to the frustration of our expectations by feeling angry or frustrated. When the expectation is that a *person* will act in a certain way, disappointment may produce the reactive attitudes, and not merely nonpersonal analogues of them.

By contrast, disappointed hope is not experienced as the loss of something to which one was entitled, and this generates "discomfort or discouragement" instead of anger.[41] This response, too, may have an analogue among the reactive attitudes. Sometimes, when we relate to people as responsible agents, we don't hold them to some minimal standard of decency; we instead hope they exceed this standard—and when they fail, we feel *let down*, but not angry or resentful. We also may feel let down rather than resentful when we have hoped someone who often fails to act decently will, just this once, do as she ought—and she fails yet again.[42] The "discomfort or discouragement" we feel when our hopes regarding the non-agential world are disappointed is something like this feeling of being let down—the world has let us down, though our hope for it had no genuine normative or interpersonal tenor.[43]

There is a parallel difference in our feelings when our expectations or hopes are fulfilled. Fulfilled expectations feel like the achievement of something to which we were "entitled," and so they produce less satisfaction than do fulfilled hopes: the fulfillment of a hope is "a real success. . . . Therefore, full joy, rather than mere relief, is the most likely reaction."[44] Analogously, we don't feel particularly impressed or proud when people manage to treat us with basic human decency—the way we normatively *expect* them to treat

---

40 Strawson, "Freedom and Resentment."

41 Miceli, "Hope: The Power of Wish and Possibility," 262.

42 Adrienne M. Martin, "Owning Up and Letting Down: The Power of Apology," *Journal of Philosophy* 107.10 (2010): 534–53.

43 Reactive or normative hope is the subject of chapter 5.

44 Miceli, "Hope: The Power of Wish and Possibility," 262.

us—but we do feel impressed or proud or admiring when they exceed this minimum standard in congruence with our hopes.

It is not entirely clear whether Miceli and Castelfranchi intend the claim that expectation involves a sense of entitlement that is missing from hope as a conceptual claim or as a hypothesis up for empirical testing. Given both their field and the fact that they independently define the two states in terms of probability assignments above and below chance, respectively, I suspect they intend an empirical claim. If I am right, then what they are proposing is that we could study people first by determining whether they estimate the chances of a desired outcome at above or below chance and then determining whether they have the relevant sense of entitlement with regard to the outcome, along with the associated affective responses to the outcome's occurrence or failure to occur.

I am willing to bet that if we were to run experiments of this kind, we would end up disconfirming the empirical hypothesis, at least in some significant populations or contexts. There are many factors determining whether we hope for or expect a desired outcome. I have already noted the probable impact of the stakes resting on the outcome. Another factor is how much an individual or her community values what we might describe as a kind of humility—how seriously do they think we ought to take uncertainty? Do they see it as reasonable or hubristic to rely on uncertain outcomes? Factors like these almost certainly do not consistently track or correlate to the relevant party's probability assignment. Instead, such factors influence how people *see* the probabilities they assign—what sorts of feelings they take those probabilities to license. If the stakes are high, or a person values humility and disapproves of risk-taking, it will be harder for her to feel legitimately "entitled" to a desired outcome. She will demand better odds before crossing from hope to expectation.

In other words, I believe Miceli and Castelfranchi provide a promising account of one element of hope. To hope is, in part, to stand ready to justify feeling anticipation (but not entitlement) when imagining the hoped-for outcome, disappointment (but not anger) if the hope is not fulfilled, and joy (rather than relief) if it is fulfilled.[45] Note that the feelings definitive of hope and the parenthetical feelings—those definitive of positive expectation—are by no means in psychological or conceptual tension with each other. Thus far, then, the incorporation analysis of hope makes sense of various people's differing linguistic intuitions about "hope" and "expect." Those who find nothing strange about asserting both hope and expectation with regard to the

---

45 We can refine this further by noting that, if the hoped-for outcome is a person's action, the relevant feelings are reactive attitudes: normative anticipation (not demand or expectation), a sense of being let down (not resentment), and pride (rather than something like normative satisfaction).

same event focus on the fact that the two attitudes involve the *same family* of thoughts and feelings; while those who find such assertions incongruous focus on the fact that hope and expectation are *distinguishable members* of this family.

Let us briefly return to the contrast between hope and despair. A person who despairs of a desired outcome in the second sense described above—that is, despair in the mind-occupying, agonizing sense—clearly does not stand ready to justify any of the feelings associated with either hope or expectation. Instead, she sees the desired outcome's probability in such a way that she stands ready to justify fantasies accompanied by gloomy feelings of depression and sadness. She adopts the stance that she should not feel disappointment if the outcome fails to occur, but only continued sadness, and perhaps a sort of perverse satisfaction (though of course being in despair does not preclude being extremely disappointed, for example, by the circumstances generating one's despair). If the desired outcome were to occur, her stance would be that she should feel not just joy, but joyful *surprise*.

One might doubt whether these feelings—anticipation, disappointment, joy—are really the sort of thing that can be *justified*. My view is that they are at least partly reason-responsive and can therefore be justified or unjustified (unlike desire/attraction, which I discuss in the next chapter). Consider, for example, the interpersonal or normative versions of these feelings, which we feel when we pin our hopes on people we see as responsible agents. When I hold out hope that this person, who has let me down so many times before, will finally see the light and decide to do what is right, I tend to feel a sense of anticipation about the outcome of her decision: a feeling of *wouldn't it be wonderful if she . . . and she might . . . but she never has before . . . .* As I will discuss in chapter 5, these are judgments (or proto-judgments) about her character, and I will normally stop making them if I believe there is good reason to. If, for example, something happens to convince me that she is thoroughly corrupt, I will feel differently: *isn't it a shame . . . she just can't or won't . . . .* When hope is not a normative attitude, when it is hope for a non-agential outcome, anticipation loses its normative tenor. But it contains non-normative judgments about the world and its processes: *wouldn't it be wonderful if . . . and it might, but . . . .* These judgments, too, are responsive to reasons; if I feel hopeful anticipation about an outcome I see as too unlikely to license this feeling, I can resist it, and instead feel: *how unfortunate . . . the world is so hard . . . ,* etc.[46]

---

46 What I say here about feelings of anticipation and so on should not be extended to desire/attraction. As I argue in the next chapter, one important human motivational state is a nonrational representation, which is not reason-responsive, and not the sort of thing for which it is appropriate to demand justification

Summary

Alan and Bess, the two phase 1 cancer research participants, strongly desire that the experimental drug will turn out to be a cure, and they agree that this outcome would be a "miracle"—the chances are less than one percent. Bess, however, has incorporated these attitudes, her desire and her probability assignment, into a justificatory rationale for hopeful feelings and activities. She stands ready to justify relying on a cure in making her future plans, though she also thinks she ought to have a back-up plan in place. She also thinks it is justifiable to spend a fair amount of time imagining scenarios related to a cure, such as good news on her next scan, or the return of health and energy. Moreover, she sees it as justifiable that, when she engages in these fantasies, she feels a positive feeling of anticipation—indeed, this is what we might call the *feeling* of hope, its occurrent affective presence.

In the original version of *Cancer Research*, I characterized Alan as hopeful but not *as* hopeful as Bess. He does not, I said, really *hope against hope*. Under the incorporation analysis, the difference is one of degree. Alan perhaps stands ready to justify some of these activities; he thinks it is reasonable to fantasize a bit about good outcomes and feel fairly positive about his fantasies. But he hesitates to go as far as Bess. That 1 percent chance, by his lights, permits a degree of hope, but it is still extremely low, and he is careful not to go too far and focus too much on the possibility of a cure.

If we change the case to one where Alan despairs, this analysis allows for two possibilities. First, given that Alan has bothered to enroll in research, the more likely scenario is that he "despairs of" a cure, but not in the mind-occupying, agonizing sense: he sees 1 percent as so low that he ought not dwell on the idea of a cure, and he certainly ought not allow himself to feel anticipation about it or rely on it in his plans. Instead, he ought to focus his mind and plans on other, more attainable outcomes, such as contributing to treatments for future cancer patients. Second, it is possible that Alan despairs in the second sense, and attaches such value to a cure that he sees it as pointless to try to get on with his life (again, though, it's hard to see how someone suffering through this kind of despair could continue to get himself to the clinic for treatments and do the other things necessary for his trial participation). In that case, he sees 1 percent in such a way that he thinks it is justifiable for him to imagine a cure and feel terrible as a result.

I leave it to the reader to extend these points to *Shawshank Redemption* and other cases with the same structure. The point here has been to provide a detailed characterization of the kinds of activities and feelings seen as justified, from the hopeful person's perspective. In the next chapter, I turn to the details of the justificatory rationale at the heart of hope.

Incorporation

The element missing from the orthodox definition of hope is a way of seeing one's situation, such that one stands ready to offer a certain kind of justificatory rationale for the forms of planning, thought, and feeling discussed in the previous chapter. This justificatory rationale is a way of incorporating certain considerations into our rational agency or scheme of ends.[1] If we add this element to the orthodox definition, we are able to explicate cases like *Cancer Research*, *Shawshank Redemption*, and *Lottery Ticket*. As I will argue at the end of this chapter, this element is also present in more prosaic forms of hope—usually in a purely dispositional form—so the incorporation analysis provides a unified account of hope, and not only an account of hoping against hope. In chapters 3 and 4, I go on to argue that this analysis is also the basis for a compelling account of how some forms of hope have a unique *sustaining power*; and, in chapter 5, I use it to argue that investing hope *in* people is also an important mode of interpersonal relation, on a par with holding people responsible.

In this chapter, I provide the details of the incorporation element, which I have until now described only sketchily. As I have indicated, this element has two parts. First, the hopeful person takes a "licensing" stance toward the probability she assigns the hoped-for outcome—she sees that probability as licensing her to treat her desire for the outcome and the outcome's desirable features as reasons to engage in the forms of planning, thought, and feeling discussed in the previous chapter. (For the sake of brevity, I will often write of seeing or representing the probability in "the licensing way.") After some scene-setting, I provide an account of this "seeing as." The second part of hope's incorporation element is the hopeful person actually treating her desire and the outcome's desirable features as reasons to engage in said forms of planning, thought, and feeling. Thus, after discussing the licensing stance, I will elucidate the difference between *desiring* an outcome in the sense of finding it attractive or compelling, and treating one's attraction as a reason.

---

1 On the term "incorporation," see chapter 1.

Together, these two discussions explain what exactly it means to say that a hopeful person *stands ready to offer a certain kind of justificatory rationale* for her hopeful plans, thoughts, and feelings. In each of these discussions, I focus on understanding these aspects of hope in terms of the most fundamental rational norms governing them. Let me begin by saying a bit about what I mean by this focus, and why I adopt it.

Understanding Mental States through Their Fundamental Norms

"Hope," using the term perhaps a bit loosely, is a mental state composed of other mental states: desire, probability assignment, the representation of the probability in a licensing way, the representation of the desire as a practical reason.[2] There are many good ways to increase our understanding of a given mental state. We can analyze it into or at least relate it to other mental states, we can think about its function in our mental economies, we can study it empirically. In the first chapter, I drew on all three of these methodologies—especially the first—in order to arrive at the incorporation analysis. I believe this analysis gets us pretty close to basic mental building blocks, and that one of the best ways to understand such basic elements is to turn to a kind of normative inquiry. This kind of inquiry aims to discover what makes a mental state the state it is, by examining when it counts as a successful or correct instance of its kind, and when it counts as defective or flawed. To make this discovery is to identify the most fundamental norms that govern the state, to establish what sorts of considerations are normatively relevant to its revision. This will be my focus in this chapter: understanding hope's various components by determining what they have to be like in order to be successful instances of their types.

Even more specifically, I will focus on the fundamental *rational* norms governing hope's components. I mean this in a fairly narrow way. I am inquiring into only the rational norms governing each element *in virtue of the kind of mental state it is*. These are general principles identifying the kinds of considerations that can provide *reasons* (hence "*rational* norms") to revise a state of that type, such that, if one is exposed to such considerations and fails to revise in the appropriate way, the state is defective. On the flip side, it is responsiveness to said considerations that makes the state a "correct" state of its type. Thus there may be other rational norms that apply to a state in a non-essential way, a way not tied to the very nature of the state and what makes it a successful or correct instance of its type—and I will not be discussing these. When I talk about a belief or some other mental state being "rational," I mean

---

2 This characterization requires using the term "mental state" somewhat loosely, because the latter two representations may be best thought of also as *activities*, at least in certain contexts.

"rational" in this sense: namely, that it is a successful instance of its type in virtue of the reasons to which it is responsive.[3]

Nevertheless, I do aim to keep my inquiry fairly broad, in the sense that I intend not to specify the potential reason-providing considerations beyond distinguishing theoretical and practical norms. By a "theoretical" norm, I mean a principle identifying considerations of *truth-approximation* as relevant to a mental state's correctness. Examples include a norm requiring that one believe a proposition only when one has decisive evidence of its truth, or a norm requiring that one suspend judgment about a proposition when the evidence for and against it is roughly in balance. By a "practical" norm, I mean a principle identifying considerations of *rational-ends-promotion* as relevant to a mental state's correctness. Examples include a norm requiring that one take the necessary means to one's rational end or abandon the end, or a norm requiring that one refrain from simultaneously having two incompatible ends.[4] My argument is that hope is governed by both theoretical and practical norms, but that the practical dominates in an important way. For clarity's sake, it may be worth anticipating my conclusions in a somewhat dry way:

1 The desire for (or what I will come to call "attraction to") the hoped-for outcome is not governed by these kinds of norms at all—it is not a state we enter or revise for reasons; it is subrational.
2 The probability assigned to the hoped-for outcome is governed exclusively by theoretical norms, or considerations of truth-approximation.
3 The representation of the probability in a licensing way is governed exclusively by practical norms, or considerations of rational-ends-promotion.
4 The representations of the desire/attraction and the outcome's desirable features as reasons to engage in certain forms of thought, planning, and feeling are governed exclusively by practical norms, or considerations of rational-ends-promotion.

The practical dominates because, although hope is beholden to considerations of truth-approximation via its constituent probability estimate, what determines whether it is correct for the hopeful person to then see that probability in the licensing way is whether it promotes her rational ends to do so. With this license in hand, the hopeful person is then free to treat her desire

---

3 Thus, there may be norms governing some states in a fundamental but not rational way—for example, it seems plausible that subrational desire/attraction is governed by a fundamental norm that says it is successful insofar as it promotes the subject's well-being. If any of the states I am examining here are fundamentally governed by both rational and nonrational norms, then what I say here describes a necessary but not sufficient condition on their success. I am not going to investigate this possibility.

4 Among practical norms are therefore the principles that tell us which (final) ends we are rationally required to have (if there are any).

for the hoped-for outcome and the outcome's desirable features as reasons to engage in fantasies about the outcome, build the outcome into her plans, and feel positive anticipation about it. She is "free" to do so in the sense that her hope is successful as the kind of state it is, so long as it promotes her rational ends to do these things.

It may be helpful to note that this conception of practical rationality as coherence with and contribution to a rational scheme of ends is closely akin to the conception Rawls draws from Kant in *Theory of Justice*.[5] According to Rawls, what makes acting on a desire rational is that it coheres with and promotes one's rational "life plan." I prefer the concept of a rational "scheme of ends" to a life plan, simply because I do not think rationality requires having anything as temporally extended as a life plan; but the general conception of practical rationality is one I would endorse. (I note, too, that there is room here to layer on additional, external theories of practical rationality—so, for example, a rationalist about moral requirements might adopt this coherentist conception of practical rationality and then add that what makes a *scheme of ends* rational is in part a matter of whether it conforms to moral requirements. I will not be defending any particular theory of what makes a scheme of ends rational, instead focusing on the core, coherentist conception of practical rationality. This makes my account of hope useful to many different philosophers, ascribing to differing theories of practical rationality.)

Two Constraints on Reasons

As noted above, my primary aim in this chapter is to provide a detailed account of hope's incorporation element. My focus will be on determining the fundamental rational norms governing this element. An account of the norms governing the other two elements—the desire and the probability assignment—will emerge en route, primarily by way of contrast. My arguments rely on two related principles that identify constraints on what kinds of considerations can provide reasons to revise a given type of mental state. I'll call these principles *Normative Governance Requires Deliberative Responsiveness* and *Deliberation Constrains Reasons*.

Normative Governance Requires Deliberative Responsiveness

To say a mental state is governed by rational norms, in the sense I specified above, is to say that it is possible for the state to be a successful or defective instance of the kind of state it is in virtue of its responsiveness or lack of

---

5 See, in particular, *A Theory of Justice*, 564, 408–409, 424–46. Thanks to Samuel Freeman and Kok Chor Tan for alerting me to this affinity.

responsiveness to reasons. By most people's lights, a false belief is a defective belief because considerations of truth-approximation provide reasons to revise beliefs, and a self-defeating intention is a flawed intention because considerations of rational-ends-promotion provide reasons to revise intentions. By most people's lights, these are thus examples of states governed by rational norms.

The principle that *Normative Governance Requires Deliberative Responsiveness* says a mental state is governed by rational norms only if it is the type of state that is responsive to reasons in a certain way: namely, only if it is possible for a person, absent confounding factors like weakness of will or cognitive confusion, to adopt, relinquish, revise, or maintain the state (hereafter, just "revise") as a direct result of deliberation about the reasons for doing so. Three points about this principle need clarifying.

First, a concept or mental state can function in the background of deliberation, without being the explicit subject.[6] So, when an agent deliberates about what to do, she may think only about the features of her options, such as the likely consequences, the means they require, how pleasant or painful they are, and so on. Nevertheless, the concept of a reason operates in the background of her deliberation; when she decides on a course of action because of some of its features, she implicitly treats those features as reasons to take that course of action. Her decision is *based on* or *commits her to* the recognition of reasons for her action. This fact generalizes to all forms of deliberation. Thus, a person may deliberate about whether to believe a proposition without ever explicitly thinking of the evidence supporting the proposition as a reason to believe p, but she still treats that evidence as reason to believe when she comes to believe the proposition on the basis of that evidence.

Second, to say a mental state is the *direct* conclusion of deliberation is to say it is *possible* for the deliberator to revise the state as the result of her recognition of the reasons in favor of it, *without the need for any intervening process* of manipulation, conditioning, habitual practice, etc. Consider two ways a person might come to believe God exists. On the one hand, I might read a well-constructed argument and become convinced the nature of the world as I find it presupposes God's existence. I thus take the nature of the world as conclusive evidence for God's existence, and I form the belief in God on this basis. On the other hand, I might read Pascal and become convinced it would be in my best interest to believe in God. I also judge this is a sufficient reason to believe in God. Famously, however, I cannot on the basis of these convictions alone come to believe in God. Instead, I need to go on *as if* I believed in God, practicing certain rituals, associating with people who believe, and so on. Eventually, if I am lucky, my own belief in God will non-deliberatively arise out of these practices.

---

6 Philip Pettit and Michael Smith, "Backgrounding Desire."

In the first case but not the second, my belief is the *direct conclusion* of my deliberation about the reasons for holding it; my belief is *based on* the reasons I take into account in my deliberation. Now, the first case demonstrates that the belief in God—or belief in general—is the type of state that *can be* the direct conclusion of deliberation, so *both* instances are governed by a rational norm or norms. That is, it is appropriate to ask of both the belief that results from the theoretical argument and the belief that results from self-manipulation in the pursuit of self-interest whether it is a successful or defective instance of belief, in virtue of its responsiveness or lack thereof to reasons. I will return to the question whether beliefs based on reasons of self-interest can be successful in this sense or are necessarily defective. For now, the important point is simply that, if a mental state is an appropriate target of evaluation in light of the fundamental rational norms governing it, it must be *possible* for it to be the *direct* conclusion of *some* form of deliberation about the reasons for adopting it.

Third, and relatedly, a mental state can be "based on reasons" in the relevant sense without actual or explicit deliberation occurring. We often adopt, modify, and abandon mental states without explicitly deliberating about it, without articulating to ourselves the reasons supporting and opposing the states. Every morning, I form and enact the intention of brushing my teeth, and the whole process happens on autopilot, so to speak. I don't run through the reasons for tooth-brushing every—or any—morning. Nor do I think there was ever a time when I considered the reasons for forming the intention to brush my teeth every morning. The practice is simply a habit that developed over time, probably starting with my parents telling me to brush my teeth in the mornings. Nevertheless, my daily adoption of the intention to brush my teeth (or my one-time adoption of the intention to brush my teeth daily) is based on reasons in the following sense: if challenged, I should be able to construct the deliberative process that would conclude with my adopting this intention. So that is part of what it means for a state to be the possible conclusion of deliberation—not that the deliberation has ever actually occurred, but that the person holding the attitude is *accountable* for being able to construct the deliberation.

Why believe *Normative Governance Requires Deliberative Responsiveness*? It is, I think, almost tautologous. Consider what it would mean if this principle were not true. Among other things, it would mean a state could be defective in virtue of its non-responsiveness to reasons even while it was impossible for an individual to revise states of that type on the basis of deliberation. Take a simple pain. It is not possible to make a pain go away *just* by deliberating about why one should not be experiencing it—say, for example, one is experiencing a "phantom" pain in an amputated limb. *Normative Governance Requires Deliberative Responsiveness* sensibly says this means the pain cannot be defective in virtue of its failure to vanish when one considers the reasons against it. The pain might be defective in other ways. It might be part of the pain's function that it is a sign of damage or potential damage, and so a phantom pain is a defective pain; it is not, however, defective in virtue of its lack of reason-responsiveness—it is just not the type of mental state that is governed by rational norms. Later in this chapter, I will argue that desire ("attraction") is another a state that is precluded from this sort of evaluation by the principle that *Normative Governance Requires Deliberative Responsiveness*. Each of hope's other elements, by contrast, satisfies this principle. In order to determine specifically what *kinds* of rational principles govern these other elements, I will rely on a further constraining principle, to which I now turn.

Deliberation Constrains Reasons

In his article, "A New Argument for Evidentialism," Nishi Shah articulates what he calls "the deliberative constraint on reasons": "R is a reason for X to φ only if R is capable of disposing X to φ in the way characteristic of R's functioning as a premise in deliberation whether to φ."[7] This principle, though clearly related to *Normative Governance Requires Deliberative Responsiveness*, is more substantive. The latter tells us what a state has to be like if it is to be the sort of thing for which we can demand reasons: it has to be the sort of state we can revise directly upon deliberating to the conclusion that it should be revised. The deliberative constraint tells us instead what a consideration has to be like if it is to be a reason for an individual to revise one of her mental states: it has to be capable of functioning as a premise in deliberation that sways the individual toward that revision.

Shah is right, I think, when he says the deliberative constraint and his argument for it follow a path laid by Bernard Williams in his classic, "Internal and External Reasons."[8] Williams' basic insight is that a reason for a person to act must be a reason *for which* that person could (in a sense to be specified below) act. Williams is focused on the idea that it has to be possible for a consideration to *motivate* a person to act if it is to count as a reason. Now, we do not, without independent argument, have the right to any assumptions about what kinds of considerations can motivate, and Williams writes in a way that is suggestive of the Humean view that only desire, a nonrational state, can motivate.[9] So Williams' argument is sometimes mistakenly interpreted as supporting antirationalist or anti-Kantian conclusions about practical reasons. In fact, however, Williams' basic insight does not by

---

7 Nishi Shah, "A New Argument for Evidentialism," *Philosophical Quarterly* 56.225 (2006): 485.

8 Bernard Williams, "Internal and External Reasons."

9 He does not in fact explicitly endorse this view, and even says at one point that the belief that one has a reason to act disposes one to action.

itself preclude any theory of motivation. As Christine Korsgaard argues, even someone who believes in a genuinely practical faculty of reason can embrace the idea that only potentially motivational considerations qualify as reasons for action—she just maintains that some purely rational considerations are potentially motivational.[10]

Moreover, we should take seriously the possibility that Williams' crucial insight isn't really about *motivation to action* at all, but rather about the concept of a reason. Namely, the insight is that the concept of a reason is the concept of a consideration by which we can *guide* ourselves—in action or in thought. Consider how Shah develops his argument for the deliberative constraint on reasons:

> Claiming that a consideration is a reason for an agent to φ implies that it is capable of being a reason for which the agent φs. Claiming that a consideration is a reason for which an agent φs in turn implies that the consideration guided the agent in its capacity as a reason. A consideration could not guide an agent to φ in its capacity as a reason unless the agent were capable of φing on the basis of his recognition of the consideration as a reason to φ. Deliberation, or reasoning, is the process in which agents recognize reasons, and then φ on the basis of this recognition. So something could not be a reason for an agent to φ unless it was capable of swaying him towards φing in his deliberation about whether to φ.[11]

φ-ing "on the basis of the recognition of a reason" to φ could be forming the intention (being motivated) to act, or it could be coming to form a belief, or it could be revising any other sort of mental state we are capable of revising as the conclusion of deliberation.[12] Williams' crucial insight is really that, for a consideration to qualify as a reason for a person to revise any mental state—a belief, an intention to act, etc.—it has to be possible for that consideration to dispose that person to that revision, and to dispose her in the manner of a reason—that is, through her recognition of that consideration as having normative authority. And that is Shah's "deliberative constraint on reasons," which I will refer to as the principle that *Deliberation Constrains Reasons*.

Some final points of clarification of this principle. First, what is the operative sense of "possibility," here? In what sense must a consideration be "capable" of disposing one to φ, if it is to count as a reason to φ? Williams

---

10   Christine M. Korsgaard, "Skepticism about Practical Reason," *Journal of Philosophy* 83.1 (1986), 5–25.

11   Nishi Shah, "A New Argument for Evidentialism," 485–86.

12   Nothing turns on the term "motivation," really. We can use the term broadly and talk about being motivated to form or revise a belief, but Williams and many of his interpreters do seem to think he has had an insight that is particular to reasons for action, in virtue of the fact that these reasons have to be capable of motivating.

argues that it must be possible for a person to deliberate (about such matters as the time-ordering of projects, constitutive solutions, the relative value of conflicting projects, and so on) from her actual "subjective motivational set" to a motive to φ. Taking a potentially broader view, Shah suggests, "The sense in which R must be capable of disposing X to φ is that there are no unalterable features of X's psychology that prevent R from disposing X to φ in the way characteristic of a consideration's functioning as a premise in deliberation about whether to φ."[13] These are both ways of constraining reasons by *psychological* possibility, and it is easy to imagine someone like Korsgaard objecting that what really matters is *rational* possibility. That is, a yet broader view would be that, to qualify as a reason for a person to φ, it must be the case that, if that person were *rational*, that consideration would, functioning as a premise in her deliberation about whether to φ, dispose her to do so. It does not matter if some "unalterable" feature of her psychology, such as a deep-seated phobia, would prevent this from happening.

It seems to me the right view is somewhere in between Shah's and the rationalist's (or perhaps it is just Shah's—he doesn't say what he means by an "unalterable" feature of a person's psychology). Consider a person with an antisocial personality disorder, incapable of being moved by considerations of others' suffering, social or moral norms, what it takes to maintain a social relationship, and so on. Her disorder is, though in some sense contingent, for all intents and purposes, inalterable. On either Williams' or Shah's view, it would seem that the consideration that an action would cause extreme suffering to another cannot be a reason for this person to refrain from that action. On at least some rationalist views, it can: for Kant, for example, moral requirements are rational requirements, and it is true that a rational individual would be motivated to refrain from causing extreme suffering.

Which of these verdicts is intuitively correct depends, I think, on how extreme a case we are imagining. For a full-on sociopath, insisting there is reason for him to behave otherwise is not just pointless, it is a conceptual misfire, and the fact that, if only he were rational, he would behave otherwise is irrelevant. For your average Bain Capital CEO, on the other hand, it is absolutely apt to insist there are reasons for him to maintain a higher standard of behavior—the fact that he is psychologically incapable of recognizing certain classes of people as people is irrelevant.[14] So there are

---

13 Shah, "A New Argument," 485.

14 So I am being bombastic and opinionated in this example. To be (slightly) less so: There are individuals who are genuinely psychologically incapable—either they were born that way or trained to it—of recognizing certain classes of people as people; and these individuals are more likely to become successful CEOs than those who, say, suffer qualms at the prospect of firing large groups of long-loyal employees. In spite of their psychological disorder, these people have reason to behave other than they do. Inalterable psychological immobility doesn't always release one from the grip of certain basic moral reasons.

certain arguably "unalterable features" of people's psychology that prevent those people from being swayed by certain kinds of considerations but that do not block those considerations from providing reasons for those people to revise their mental states. Yet there are other such features that do. For my purposes going forward, it is not necessary to have an account of what distinguishes these two kinds of features, but only to mark that there are these two kinds.

A second point to clarify about *Deliberation Constrains Reasons* is that, as with *Normative Governance Requires Deliberative Responsiveness*, it does not commit us to an especially reflective or self-conscious picture of how we actually deliberate about and respond to reasons. A consideration can provide a reason for one to revise a mental state even if one never actually reflects on the consideration or is never either consciously or unconsciously swayed by it. It only need be possible (in the sense discussed above) for one to take it up into deliberation and be swayed by it. And if one does "take it up into deliberation," it need not be the case that this deliberation is explicit or articulated at the conscious level; when one acts (or believes, etc.) on the basis of a consideration, in the sense that one would offer up that consideration as part of a justification—a justification that would be the reconstruction of a deliberative process concluding in the decision to act as one did—then one has "taken it up into deliberation" in the relevant sense.

The Licensing Stance

With *Deliberation Constrains Reasons* in hand (I will rely on *Normative Governance Requires Deliberative Responsiveness* later, in discussing desire) we are ready to turn to the details of hope's incorporation element. We can separate this element into two attitudes or stances: an attitude toward one's own attraction to the hoped-for outcome, according to which it *qualifies as a reason* to engage in hopeful plans, thoughts, and feelings; and an attitude toward the probability assigned to the hoped-for outcome, according to which it *allows* one's attraction to so qualify. The second attitude is what I will call the "licensing stance," and it treats a probability as an "enabling condition" for a reason.[15] In the next section, I will explain what is involved in the first attitude—that is, what it means to treat a consideration as a practical reason. In this section, I discuss the nature of the licensing stance. I will argue that it is a practical as opposed to theoretical attitude, but that it is not intrinsically motivational; rather, adopting it enables the adoption of a further, intrinsically motivational attitude.

15 On the concept of an "enabling condition," see Jonathan Dancy, *Practical Reality* (Oxford: Clarendon Press, 2000).

Two people find the same outcome equally compelling, and both agree it is extraordinarily unlikely. One looks at the situation and says, "I grant you it is *possible*, but the chance is only one in a thousand!" The other says, "I grant you the chance is only one in a thousand, but it is *possible*!" What is this difference in their attitudes? I attempt here to articulate the difference in a way that does not presuppose any particular theory or analysis of subjective probabilities. The crucial idea captured in this scenario is the possibility of, on the one hand, committing to some probability-related *description* of a situation and, on the other hand, *evaluating* the situation so-described in a way that makes it practically relevant in a broad way—that is, relevant to how one thinks one should *feel* about the situation, *think* about it, and/or *structure one's plans* in relation to it. Some theories of subjective probability want to treat it as an essentially practical attitude, and they will prefer to call the probability-related description of the situation something other than a "subjective probability assignment"—perhaps it is just a nod to what the experts say, for example.[16] Others line up more with what I take to be common pre-theoretic linguistic intuitions, and will give the label "probability assignment" to the probability-related description, while considering the way one evaluates the situation so-described a way of seeing one's probability assignment. I am going to talk in a way that accords with the latter sort of view, but I do not think much turns on this choice of vocabulary.

With this in mind, let's give a little more substance to the difference we are examining. Say cancer research participants Alan and Bess accept the same probability-related description of the outcome where they are cured by the experimental drug (hereafter: they assign the same probability to this outcome). Even with this similarity, they differ on how much mental energy they are willing to dedicate to thoughts of a cure, whether they are comfortable with feelings of anticipation, and whether they are willing to rely on a cure in their plans for the future. These differences are indications of the underlying stances they take toward the probability. There are many ways one can describe or frame a probability that will dispose one to display these kinds of differences. As we've seen, we can describe a very small probability as exactly that, or we can emphasize that it is within the realm of possibility—that it is "not impossible." A 0.52 probability can be "a better than even chance" or "hardly better than an even chance." Odds of 1 to 770,000 can be "about as likely as getting struck by lightning this year,"[17] or "*way* more likely than winning the lottery."[18] A 0.4 probability can be "40 percent," "2 out of 5," a

16 See for example, P. F. Ramsey, "Truth and Probability," in *Studies in Subjective Probability*, 2nd ed., Henry E. Kyburg and Howard E. K. Smokler, eds. (Huntington, NY: Robert E. Kreiger, 1980), 23–52.

17 For National Weather Service Storm Data, see: http://www.lightningsafety.noaa.gov/medical.htm.

18 For a standard 6 in 49 game, the odds of winning are 1 in 13,983,816.

picture of two cherries and three lemons, or a picture of five stick figures with three X-ed out.

Now, the representation of a probability *can* affect a person's subjective probability assignment. So, for example, if she is told simply that the odds of an outcome are 1:770,000 and then asked what probability she assigns to it, she may stick with 1:770,000; but, if then told that it is about as likely as getting struck by lightning, she may adjust downward; or, if told it is "*way* more likely than winning the lottery," upward. It is also possible, however, that her probability assignment will remain fixed, while her thoughts, feelings, and plans will adjust: the comparison to lightning may not change the probability she assigns, but it may lead her to try to turn her attention to other matters or to resist feelings of warm anticipation, and it may dissuade her from making any plans reliant on winning, while the comparison to the lottery has the opposite effect. In the latter set of cases, the different representations constitute the stance she adopts toward the outcome's probability, and what she sees that probability as licensing.

The crucial difference between a subjective probability assignment and representing a probability in the licensing way is that the first is a theoretical attitude, while the second is a practical one. That is to say, a subjective probability assignment is successful or defective as a subjective probability assignment exclusively in virtue of its responsiveness to considerations of truth-approximation; while a licensing stance taken toward a probability assignment is successful or defective as a licensing stance exclusively in virtue of its responsiveness to considerations of rational ends promotion. That is what I will argue in the next three sections.

The Transparency of Doxastic Deliberation to Evidence

As we saw above, it is psychologically possible for the belief in God to be the conclusion of deliberation about the reasons for believing in God. The relevant deliberative process focuses on the evidence for the truth of the proposition that God exists. If the deliberator determines there is adequate evidence God exists, she will believe God exists on this basis (assuming no psychological noise or breakdown in her rational capacities). By contrast, it is not psychologically possible to reach the belief in God as the direct conclusion of deliberation about its pragmatic value. In the literature on belief, this phenomenon is known as the "transparency" of belief-formation—or, more specifically, doxastic deliberation—to evidence.[19] As Shah puts it, "[T]he

<hr />

19 In addition to Shah, "A New Argument," see R. Moran, "Making Up Your Mind: Self-Interpretation and Self-Constitution," *Ratio*, NS I (1988), 135–51; and J. David Velleman and Nishi Shah, "Doxastic Deliberation," *Philosophical Review* 114.4 (October 2005): 497–534.

deliberative question of *whether to believe that p* inevitably gives way to the factual question *whether p*, because the answer to the latter question will determine the answer to the former."[20]

Now, as discussed above, concepts and attitudes are often "backgrounded" in deliberation.[21] We often do not explicitly take the fact *that we believe p* into account when deliberating, and instead rely on simply the proposition that *p*. And we often do not explicitly deliberate about whether *to believe* that *p*; we deliberate instead about whether *p*. We are, however, capable of entertaining the former question. The point about transparency is that, when we do entertain the question whether to believe *p*, we answer it in virtue of answering the question whether *p*, where belief is backgrounded. In other words, the only considerations we take into account when deliberating about whether to believe that *p* are considerations that directly support or oppose the truth of *p*. This is supposed to be a psychological truth, an observation of our psychological capacities in doxastic deliberation. Considered by itself, the transparency of belief does not rule out the possibility that nonevidential considerations can be reasons to believe or disbelieve that *p*; it is possible that considerations we are incapable of incorporating into deliberation determine the success or correctness of some beliefs. Returning to Pascal's wager, all transparency says is that I cannot produce in myself the belief in God by deliberating in terms of the wager. I will have to resort to nondeliberative means to induce this belief.

That is to say, this observation about the transparency of doxastic deliberation to evidence is consistent with the equally true observation that other, nonevidential considerations often influence our beliefs through other, nondeliberative processes. So, let us turn now to the probability-related descriptions I have been calling "subjective probability estimates." It seems reasonable also to call them "partial beliefs," precisely because deliberation about them, too, is transparent to evidence of their truth or accuracy. To emphasize: The point is that when we *deliberate* about what probability to assign to an outcome, or what degree of belief to invest in it, we are psychologically limited to considerations of truth-approximation or accurate prediction, such as: what do the experts say? what has my experience of similar situations been in the past? what else has to happen for this outcome to occur, and how likely is that? One can, of course, decide that because the pay-off would be so great, one is willing to invest a lot in an extremely unlikely outcome—but then one has moved on to what I previously called a practical *evaluation* of the probability-related description one endorses.[22]

20   Shah, "A New Argument," 481–82.

21   Pettit and Smith, "Backgrounding Desire." See below for further discussion.

22   Again, some probability theorists will call this willingness to invest a "subjective probability assignment," but this is just a difference in vocabulary.

Putting Transparency and Deliberation Constrains Reasons Together

Shah and others have pointed out that, if deliberation about whether to believe a proposition is psychologically transparent to considerations relevant to the truth of the proposition, and deliberation constrains reasons, then the only considerations that qualify as reasons to revise a belief are considerations of truth-approximation.[23] In particular, the fact of transparency and the principle that *Deliberation Constrains Reasons* together rule out any non-evidential considerations—for example, pragmatic considerations or considerations of self-interest—as potential reasons for belief. Again, this argument extends to subjective probability assignments: the only considerations that count as reasons to assign a particular probability are those that provide evidence of the probability's accuracy. Whether a subjective probability assignment is correct as a subjective probability assignment is determined exclusively by whether it is based on the best evidence available to the person making the assignment. That is to say, the fundamental rational norm(s) governing probability assignments identify exclusively considerations of truth-approximation as relevant to the assignments' correctness.[24]

Practical Deliberation about the Licensing Stance

So far, I have argued that, when a person assigns a probability to an outcome, she thereby adopts an attitude governed exclusively by a norm requiring responsiveness to considerations of truth-approximation. In short, this attitude—including when it is an element of hope—is a mental state governed exclusively by what I have called a "theoretical" rational norm.[25] Now I want to underscore how different the "licensing stance" is: whether one sees an outcome's probability in the licensing way is, at a fundamental normative level, a *practical* matter; the fundamental rational norm governing this mental state requires responsiveness to considerations of rational ends-promotion rather than truth-approximation.

As before, my argument runs via the implications of *Deliberation Constrains Reasons* when combined with psychological observations about

23   Shah, "A New Argument"; Velleman and Shah, "Doxastic Deliberation." See also Ralph Wedgewood, "The Aim of Belief," *Philosophical Perspectives* 16: "Language and Mind" (2002): 267–97, for an argument that aiming at the truth is a constitutive norm for belief formation.

24   One must give up either the deliberative constraint or transparency in order to avoid this conclusion. Shah further argues that the deliberative constraint is part of the best explanation for transparency, leaving the pragmatist with only the option to give up both.

25   Thus we have reached conclusion #2, anticipated at the beginning of this chapter.

deliberation. It is psychologically possible to adopt the licensing stance on the basis of deliberation about how useful it would be to see things as that stance dictates. This is easiest to observe in cases of hoping against hope. In these cases, the hopeful person finds a way to emphasize the fact that an extremely low probability outcome is nevertheless in the range of *possibility*. This person focuses on possibility versus impossibility, rather than high versus low probability. Most people are capable, at least some of the time, of adopting this focus on the basis of pragmatic considerations. If such a person's deliberative processes were fully explicit and articulated, it would sound something like this: *I'm facing incredibly bad odds, but if I focus on this fact, I'm going to be paralyzed by despair. I won't be able to go on, to do what I can with the resources left to me, or to at least try to fight the odds. So I'd best not think about how poor the odds are, and instead focus on the fact that they are in the realm of possibility; nothing is certain, "miracles" happen, and so it is possible that I will get what I so desperately desire.*[26] And then she proceeds to see her situation as she has concluded she needs to see it. Or so it seems to me she might. I am not saying that this is an easy thing to do, or that she will be able to unshakably maintain the necessary stance at all times. Nevertheless, shifting our perspective on the probabilities we assign to desired outcomes is something we can learn to do in response to practical considerations.

Compare the classic cases of "seeing-as," such as seeing a painting as a landscape. Consider in particular seeing a very abstract painting—a painting that does not obviously offer itself as anything but a set of layered washes of color—as a landscape. On the first several viewings, the painting may never appear as anything but those washes of color. With some effort, however, or perhaps with some instruction, the viewer can learn to see the landscape in the layers. She learns to apply certain concepts to the shapes in the painting—this bump is a *hill*, this smooth area *a lake*—and she learns also how to see the painting via this application of concepts. Once she has this know-how, she can shift between seeing it as only washes of color and seeing it as a landscape. Moreover, she can shift *in response to practical considerations*. If someone offers her a reward to see it as a landscape, she can do so. Thus, if it is rational for her to take the means to getting the reward, it is rational for her to see the painting as a landscape. This is in contrast with both belief and desire—famously, even if believing a proposition or desiring an outcome is the only means to a fabulous reward, one cannot on this basis form the necessary belief or desire.

Similarly, there is probably a particular know-how involved in shifting one's focus from a hoped-for outcome's low probability to its possibility. One

---

26 Although there is some similarity between this rationale and Pettit's cognitive resolve, the former does not mean putting the "poor odds" off-line, but seeing them in a way that points up not their poverty but their possibility.

might need to train oneself to ignore the specific odds one has assigned and instead to think about the outcome simply in terms of possibility. And the same goes for thinking about a probability by comparing it with lightning or the lottery; one needs to know both to apply the relevant concepts and how to see the situation via that application.

Thus, *Deliberation Constrains Reasons* does not have the same implications for the licensing stance as it does for subjective probability assignments. We are psychologically capable of revising a licensing stance toward a probability assignment in response to deliberation about instrumental or practical considerations, so such considerations can qualify as reasons to revise our stance. Indeed, once we parse the two attitudes originally described at the beginning of this chapter—the probability-related description of one's situation and one's evaluation of the situation so-described for practical purposes—it appears that practical considerations are the *only* ones relevant to deliberation about the latter. The licensing stance, then, is governed *exclusively* by what I have called "practical" fundamental norms of rationality. The deliberation in question is about what one should *do* with the information contained in the probability-related description—and that is a basic practical question.

Now, I expect many readers will have no trouble accepting that the licensing stance is governed by a fundamental practical norm—but there may be some question as to whether it is governed *exclusively* by such a norm. One might arrive at this question from two directions. First, it might seem implausible that *seeing-as*, which I have used as an analogy for the licensing stance, isn't beholden to norms of accuracy. Even if different people can rationally see the same thing in different ways, surely it is not rational to see just *anything* as *anything*, even if doing so promotes rational ends! Could it possibly be entirely rational to see the duck-rabbit as a lamppost, even if one were somehow capable of doing so and were going to receive a million dollars for it?

My answer is that it might be *weird* but nevertheless, yes, entirely rational— at least potentially. There are no theoretical norms of rationality governing seeing-as; a practically rational way of seeing something is a fully rational one. However, there are potentially many ways to be practically irrational. It could be irritating or even offensive to an artist or her students to see her work in a way opposite to what she intended. It could be morose to see everything as an omen of ill fortune. And these could be failures of rationality— there might be decisive reasons for us to avoid being offensive, irritating, or morose. A way of seeing has to genuinely promote a *rational end* in order to be practically rational. If one's end is irrational, then the fact that a way of seeing promotes that end says nothing in favor of its rationality. And whether an end is rational depends on substantive norms of practical rationality. So in order to know whether a particular way of seeing is rational, we do need a substantive theory of practical rationality. For the purpose of understanding the general structure and fundamental norms governing the licensing stance, however, we can remain agnostic about what sorts of considerations provide or constitute practical reasons. Are we rationally required to follow moral norms, norms of prudence, norms of etiquette? If so, then a way of seeing that promotes an immoral, imprudent, or rude end is also irrational.[27]

The second way one might come to doubt the purely practical nature of the licensing stance is by recognizing that it would hardly be rational to adopt the stance toward a probability assignment of either 0 or 1. It is just crazy, clearly, to be hopeful in the ways described about an outcome one believes has literally no chance of occurring or that one believes is certain to occur. Observe, though, that we do not need to appeal to theoretical norms to reveal the potential for irrationality here. Consider the case of the 0 probability outcome. First, there might be some practical benefit in, say, the occasional brief fantasy about the outcome. So, if the licensing stance one adopts is specifically that the 0 probability licenses these thoughts, there is no reason to think it rationally defective. These practical benefits are pretty quickly trumped, however, by the waste of time and energy, so there has to be a low ceiling on what the rational person sees as licensed. Moreover, it is certainly practically irrational to rely on an outcome to which one (rationally) assigns 0 probability, even with a hedging back-up plan in place. So a hope that involves seeing a 0 probability as licensing this sort of planning activity is to that extent defective.

Consider next the outcome to which one assigns a probability of 1. Again, there might be some practical benefit to minimal hopeful thoughts and feelings dedicated to such an outcome, but the ceiling has to be pretty low—it would be more beneficial to spend one's thoughts and feeling elsewhere. Moreover, adopting the licensing stance constitutive of hope means seeing the outcome's probability as licensing only *hedged* plans, and it is almost certainly irrational to spend effort on backing up a plan that is certain to succeed—it would be better, practically speaking, to outright *rely* on such an outcome.

So, although it may be "just crazy" to be hopeful in the ways described about an outcome one believes has literally no chance of occurring or that one believes is certain to occur, this fact is explained by the *practical* nature of the fundamental norm governing the licensing stance. There is no need to explain away the appearance that deliberation about this stance must, psychologically and normatively speaking, focus on considerations of rational-ends-promotion. The licensing stance is fundamentally governed by a practical norm; whether it is successful or defective as the kind of state that it is depends on its responsiveness to considerations of rational-ends-promotion.

---

27 When I say an act is "rationally required," I just mean that there are decisive reasons to perform it.

The licensing stance is a practical, but not intrinsically motivational, state of mind. It is governed exclusively by a practical norm, even though it does not itself move us to make the world fit it. In a sense, then, it is an interesting challenge to the standard first distinction in taxonomies of human psychology—that is, the distinction between "cognitive" and "conative" states. The licensing stance does not aim to "fit the world," exactly. In adopting it, one does, certainly, aim to represent the probability of the hoped-for outcome in a way that allows one to act sensibly within the world, but that is not the same as aiming for accurate representation of the world when there are non-pragmatic standards of accuracy available, as in the case of belief. Nor, however, does the licensing stance aim to make the world fit it, exactly. It instead clears the way for the agent to deploy other representations that aim to change the world. If my arguments regarding the licensing stance are sound, then, we would do well to consider alternative first cuts to make in our psychologies. One candidate is between states governed by practical norms and those governed by theoretical norms; another is between non-motivational and motivational states. We needn't settle on one or the other for all purposes, either. Different taxonomies can serve different purposes. In the discussion so far, I have emphasized the differences between attitudes governed by practical versus theoretical norms. In what follows, I want to turn our attention to commonalities and differences among *motivational* representations, which are presumably governed by practical norms.

The Other Part of the Incorporation Element: Treating Desire as a Practical Reason

As I noted above, seeing probability in a licensing way does not mean seeing the probability itself as *providing* practical reasons. It rather means seeing the probability as *licensing other considerations* to provide reasons. It is giving oneself permission to treat those considerations as practical reasons. Specifically, it is giving oneself permission to treat one's *desire* for the hoped-for outcome, and the outcome's desirable features, as reasons.

A terminological note: at this point, I want to set aside the term "desire," because it has a lot of philosophical baggage. I aim to identify a very specific kind of motivational representation, which has a lot in common with what many people call "desire" (also "inclination"). This kind of representation is also very different from what many other people call "desire," and I am not invested in defending any particular theory of "desire;" so I will instead use the term "attraction" (and its opposite, "aversion"), and I will also sometimes talk of finding an outcome "compelling." Why I consider this vocabulary suggestive should emerge in the following discussion.

From the perspective of a deliberating agent, it is possible to find an outcome attractive or compelling while denying there is any reason to pursue that same outcome. It is possible, even, to find an outcome *overwhelmingly* attractive, so that one is unable to resist pursuing it, while nonetheless denying there is any reason to do so. Of particular significance for my purposes here is that one can treat *an attraction itself* as a practical reason, or one can deny it that status. When I am attracted to an outcome—say, my having more coffee to drink—my mind is drawn toward the thought of coffee. I keep thinking about the warmth and taste of coffee, the current emptiness of the mug, and so on. Whether I will decide to go get more coffee, however, remains an open question. I may decide this attraction to coffee is reason to drop everything and go to the kitchen *now*; or I may instead decide finishing the thought I am in the middle of writing is more important, and thus decide I will succumb to the attraction only after I have finished the paragraph; or I may decide this attraction is due to a problematic aversion to working for an extended period of time, and thus decide I will succumb to it only if it persists after an hour has passed.

The point here is one emphasized by contemporary Kantian moral philosophers: we have the capacity for reflective distance from our attractions, and deciding to act on an attraction is not the same as being moved by the strongest attraction of the moment, or even by a second-order attraction. Instead, deciding to act on an attraction is giving it normative authority, representing it—perhaps in cahoots with some other considerations—as providing sufficient reason to take some available means, or to try to make some means available. The capacity to find an outcome attractive or compelling and the capacity to treat an attraction—or any other consideration—as a practical reason are distinct motivational resources. The first is, I will say, "subrational," both because it does not make use of the concept of a justifying reason and because it is not governed by rational norms (I will say more about each of these points below). The second is "rational" both in the sense that it makes use of this concept and in the sense that it is governed by rational norms. (It is not, however, "rational" in the sense that it necessarily satisfies those norms. The agent who acts from this rational motivation stands ready to offer justification for her action, even though she may be mistaken about whether her action is actually justified.)

A sidenote: Non-Kantians often find this way of talking about motivation objectionably "reflective" or "high-order." Do we really "decide to act on" our attractions? However, the Kantian description is really a rational reconstruction of a process that is often unreflective and inarticulate at the conscious level. The point is that, viewed from a first-person perspective, there is a difference between *being moved directly* by an attraction in a fully passive way, and *treating that attraction as a reason*. The difference is not often before our minds in the moment of decision (indeed, "decision" itself is not often before our minds in the moment of decision). Rather it is a matter of what kind of accountability we implicitly accept—or for what we are normatively "on the hook." If a person is just directly moved by an attraction, then she is not disposed to appeal to that attraction when called to defend her decision, and it would be a mistake to treat her as normatively committed to the attraction. If, on the other hand, she treats it as a reason, then she is disposed to offer it up as part of the justification for her decision, and she is also normatively on the hook for doing so.

The idea that humans have both rational and subrational motivational resources has ancient roots. It is also at the heart of Kant's action theory. Plato and Aristotle believe we have distinct motivational faculties, one rational and one subrational.[28] Kant believes we have a single faculty that deploys two distinct motivational representations. I suspect that, in the end, either theory can underwrite the analysis of hope I am defending. Here, I rely on the Kantian theory.[29] The two rivals to this kind of theory are an anti-rationalist and a fully rationalist theory. Neither is adequate to explicate the observation above, regarding the experiential difference between being attracted to an outcome and deciding one's attraction is or is not a reason to pursue the outcome. To do that, we need a theory with both rational and nonrational elements.

The Inadequacy of Monist Theories of Motivation

The first, antirationalist theory is usually attributed to David Hume, although it is not exclusively the purview of Hume or his philosophical descendants. For example, Locke held a version of this view. Regardless, the view is most

---

28   Actually, they believe we have three motivational faculties: Reason, Appetite, and Spirit. Spirit is supposed to "partake of" reason, but is not itself a rational faculty—rather it is reason's enforcer. Note, too, that rational motivation is probably, for Plato and Aristotle, more closely tied to objective justification than is the form of rational motivation I describe above.

29   I have found all of the following extremely helpful in piecing together this account of a Kantian action theory: Kelly Sorensen, "Kant's Taxonomy of the Emotions," *Kantian Review* 6 (2002): 109–28; Paul Guyer, "Moral Feelings in the *Metaphysics of Morals*," in *Kant's Metaphysics of Morals: A Critical Guide,* Lara Denis, ed. (Cambridge: Cambridge University Press, 2010), 130–51; Barbara Herman, "The Will and Its Objects," *Moral Literacy* (Cambridge, MA: Harvard University Press, 2007), 230–53. Tamar Schapiro, "The Nature of Inclination"; and Andrews Reath, "Hedonism, Heteronomy and Kant's Principle of Happiness," *Agency and Autonomy in Kant's Moral Theory* (Oxford and New York: Oxford University Press, 2006), 33–66. Also, the following have helped me think about how different forms of motivation rely on different representational resources: Victoria McGeer and Philip Pettit, "The Self-Regulating Mind," *Language and Communication* 22, (2002), 281–99; and Elisabeth Camp, "Putting Thoughts to Work: Concepts, Systematicity and Stimulus-Dependence," *Philosophy and Phenomenological Research* 78.2 (2009) 275–311.

widely known as the "Humean theory of motivation."[30] Most recent proponents of the Humean theory use the term "desire" to refer to a disposition to act for the sake of bringing about a desired outcome, along with a set of supportive dispositions such as the disposition to have positive thoughts and feelings about the outcome, and to attend to the outcome's positive features.

Now, it is possible to provide a dispositional analysis of both attraction and deciding an attraction is a reason for action. The difference lies in the mechanisms by which the dispositions manifest. Attraction never directly manifests as action for the sake of the attractive outcome, though it may directly manifest as compulsive behavior that the agent neither explicitly nor implicitly endorses as justifiable. The point observed above is that, from the perspective of the deliberating agent, one must take an endorsing attitude—at the dispositional level, and in the sense that one is normatively on the hook—toward an attraction before it manifests as action for the sake of the attractive outcome. The Humean theory does not include space for this mechanism. Action is, instead, the product of a single kind of motivational representation: in the simplest version, action simply follows from the strongest "desire." This is an oversimplification, because Humeans needn't think desires compete only in terms of strength. We can also form higher-order desires that may undermine or enable lower-order desires. However, these higher-order desires don't have any justificatory content missing from lower-order desires; finding an attraction attractive doesn't invest it with any normative authority, as far as the deliberating agent is concerned.[31]

Humeans often say an agent's desire for an outcome, along with her belief that acting in a certain way will promote that outcome, "rationalizes" her acting in that way. By this, they mean that attributing the belief-desire pair to the agent establishes her action as an intentional piece of behavior.[32] They do not mean, however, that the act is, in virtue of its relation to the belief-desire pair, "rational" in a more robust sense—namely in the sense that the agent stands ready to justify it to others (or even to herself). For Humeans, determining whether an act is justified always requires referring to independent norms of desire and action—instrumental norms, such as that one should desire the means to satisfying extant desires, or that one should maximize one's overall desire-satisfaction; moral norms, such as that one should satisfy only desires that are not harmful to others; and so on. The problem is that these norms are intrinsically motivationally inert—the fact that getting more coffee will detract from my overall desire-satisfaction by delaying the completion of my work leaves me cold, unless I desire to

---

30   See Smith, "The Humean Theory of Motivation"; and Williams, "Internal and External Reasons."

31   Gary Watson, "Free Agency," *Journal of Philosophy* 72 (April 1975): 205–20.

32   Donald Davidson, "Actions, Reasons, and Causes," *Journal of Philosophy* 60.23 (1963): 685–700.

maximize my desire-satisfaction. And, even if I do, then my desire for coffee and my desire to maximize my desire-satisfaction are on all fours; there is nothing to give the latter authority over the former. What this means is that, from my perspective, it is not possible to desire a refill *now* more strongly than maximizing my desire-satisfaction, and yet resist the former for the sake of the latter.

Relatedly, Humeans are welcome to the concept of a justificatory reason, but they must see it as intrinsically motivationally inert. I can think my desire is no reason to get coffee, but this thought alone has no power to counteract that desire. I must desire acting only when I think there is reason to, if this thought is to get a motivational grip on me. This is not an entirely far-fetched interpretation of my struggle, but it does not truly fit the contours of the experience of the agent who questions the justificatory status of one of her desires.

The second rival theory of human motivation, a fully rationalist one, has its roots in the ancient Stoics,[33] and was carried on into the seventeenth century by Baruch Spinoza.[34] Most recently, T. M. Scanlon and Derek Parfit have been strong advocates for such a theory.[35] According to this theory, all motivation is *reason-driven*. When an agent deliberates, she weighs the reasons for and against the course of action she is considering. These reasons are considerations she could invoke in justifying her action to others. Of course an agent can be mistaken about whether a given consideration really is a reason to act or refrain from acting in the way she is considering; nonetheless, when she concludes her deliberation with a choice, she reaches a conclusion about what she has decisive reason to do and, normally, that is what she will do. As Scanlon writes:

> A rational person who judges there to be sufficient grounds for believing that P normally has that belief, and this judgment is normally sufficient explanation for so believing. There is no need to appeal to some further source of motivation such as "wanting to believe." Similarly, a rational person who judges there to be compelling reason to do A normally forms the intention to do A, and this judgment is sufficient explanation of the intention and of the agent's acting on it.[36]

Both belief and intention (or what I've been calling "choice" or "decision") are "judgment-sensitive attitudes"—specifically, they are sensitive or responsive

33 Stob. 2.7.10 (W 2.88); Seneca, *On Anger* 1.8.3.

34 Baruch Spinoza, *Ethics*, 2p48–49. See also Edwin Curley, "Descartes, Spinoza, and the Ethics of Belief," in *Spinoza: Essays in Interpretation*, E. Freeman and M. Mandelbaum, eds. (La Salle, IL: Open Court), 159–89.

35 Scanlon, *What We Owe to Each Other,* and Parfit, *On What Matters.*

36 Scanlon, *What We Owe to Each Other,* 33–34.

to judgments about what there is reason to believe or do. This is how deliberation is reason-driven.

According to the fully rationalist theory, there is no form of motivation other than the reason-judgments that feature in deliberation. So what of "desire"? Desire, Scanlon argues, is really the perception, or apparent perception, of reasons. All motivation is thus reason-driven, and "desire" is no exception. There is no finding an outcome attractive or compelling without thereby treating it as something there is reason to pursue. There may be ways of representing reasons that have more of a "feel" to them than others, but they are not different in kind; Scanlon calls desires with a substantial occurrent presence desires "in the directed-attention sense":

> Desire in the directed-attention sense characterizes an important form of variability in the motivational efficacy of reasons, but it does this by describing one way in which the thought of something as a reason can present itself rather than by identifying a motivating factor that is independent of such a thought.[37]

The fully rationalist theory is even worse off than the Humean theory in its inability to account for the experience of the agent who stands away from her attractions to consider whether she should be moved by them. It is worse off because it denies there is any motivational state from which we can stand back and ask, "Is this a reason to act?" If I desire more coffee, that means I represent coffee as something there is reason to drink. It is not possible for me to simultaneously represent coffee this way and to withhold judgment as to, or to ask whether there is any reason at all for me to drink more coffee. Even if there are different ways for "the thought of something as a reason" to present itself to the deliberating agent, all motivation implies the work of a justificatory concept; so there is no possibility of asking oneself whether one's motivation provides any justification. (One could ask whether it provides sufficient or decisive justification, but its presence implies that one sees at least some justification for acting as one is motivated.)

In order to make sense of the deliberating agent's experience, of the possibility of being both attracted to an outcome and asking oneself whether one's attraction provides any reason to pursue the outcome, we need a *dualist* theory of human motivation. That is, we need a theory that posits two distinct motivational capacities or representations, one with justificatory content and one without. One such theory is a Kantian one.[38]

---

37   Ibid., 40. Compare Schapiro, "Desires as Demands," *Philosophy and Phenomenological Research* 81.1 (2010): 229–236.

38   The view I develop here is drawn from Kant and indebted to the views of several contemporary Kantians (see n29, above). It is not, however, *Kant's* view in its entirety: in particular, it does

The Dualist Theory: Subrational and Rational Motivational Representations

According to Kant, when we humans are motivated, we are exercising a causal power he calls the "faculty of desire." As Kant defines it, the faculty of desire is an active power of representation. Specifically, it is a causal power that works through representation: the activity of this faculty is "the self-determination of a subject's power through the representation of something in the future as an effect of this representation."[39] Thus, any animal motion other than the reflexive (e.g., the knee-jerk reflex) or autonomic (e.g., pupil-dilation) is the product of the faculty of desire.

The content of a "desire" depends on the animal's representational resources. My dog and I may both desire a piece of cheese, but I am capable of two levels of desire, so to speak, while Zadie is limited to one. She is capable only of representing the cheese as attractive or compelling—let's follow Tamar Schapiro and say Zadie represents the cheese as *to-be-eaten*.[40] I, too, may represent the cheese as *to-be-eaten*, but I may also represent it as *something there is reason for me to eat*. Zadie is capable only of subrational representation, while I am also capable of rational representation. The latter representation has a justificatory content that is missing from the former; to say there is reason to do something is to offer it up "second-personally," as Stephen Darwall puts it[41]—that is, the concept of a reason presupposes the possibility of an exchange of justification with another individual who cares about justification. What Kant calls the "rational will" or "practical reason" is the faculty of desire motivating via rational representation. What he calls "inclination"—and I have been calling finding an outcome "attractive" or "compelling"—is the faculty of desire motivating via subrational representation.[42]

When the faculty of desire motivates via rational representation, Kant says the agent *adopts a maxim* or *sets an end*. A maxim is a representation of an end as sufficient reason to act—to take measures to acquire, protect, promote, support, develop, etc. . . . the object (depending on the nature of the

---

not rely on the notion that we make a noumenal choice between fundamental maxims of self-love or morality, or on the possibility of transcendental freedom.

39 Immanuel, Kant, *Anthropology, History and Education* (Cambridge: Cambridge University Press, 2007), 7:251.

40 Schapiro, "Desire as Demands."

41 Stephen Darwall, *The Second-Person Standpoint: Morality, Respect, and Accountability* (Cambridge, MA: Harvard University Press, 2006).

42 Kant himself apparently believed that motivation via concepts implies motivation via the concept of a reason. I see no cause to accept this assumption, however. Surely there could be motivational concepts without the justificatory content of a reason. For an argument regarding nonhuman animals' use of concepts, see Elisabeth Camp, "Putting Thoughts to Work."

object and the features that make it an end). All of the human behaviors we call "actions"—that is, all behaviors for which it is not a misfire to ask for justification in terms of reasons—are the effects of the rational will setting ends, although of course this end-setting need not be explicit or articulated. When a behavior is the direct effect of a *sub*rational representation, by contrast, it is not an action in this sense. Examples are angrily taking a swing at someone, jumping for joy, fearfully snatching the child away from the street, impulsively throwing one's arms around one's beloved. In these examples, *sub*rational attractions or "inclinations" move us directly. The actors do not stand ready to offer justification for what they do, and there is a sense in which we have misunderstood the behavior, if we expect them to be able to justify it. Of course, we may expect people to control themselves, not to allow their subrational attractions to cause them to do harmful things. So it can be appropriate to demand justification for failures of self-control—but this is demanding justification for a rational activity or its absence.

Behavior caused directly by subrational attraction is not fundamentally governed by rational norms—it is not the sort of thing apt for justification in terms of reasons—because *subrational attraction itself floats free of such norms.*[43] Here, there is an important contrast with both belief and the licensing stance. The psychological phenomenon that doxastic deliberation is transparent to evidence—that it is possible to deliberate to belief only on the basis of evidence and not on the basis of a belief's contribution to pragmatic outcomes or the believer's interests—is a sign of a deeper conceptual truth about the activity of forming belief; by its nature, belief is governed by a theoretical norm of truth-approximation. One can adopt the licensing stance, by contrast, on the basis of its contribution to one's further ends. The licensing stance is a fundamentally *practical* attitude: it is governed by a practical norm of rational-ends-promotion.

Attraction functions very differently in our psychology: it is psychologically *impossible* to become attracted to an outcome—or to revise an attraction—on the basis of deliberation *at all.* You can deliberate all you want about why you should be attracted to sitting down and working, rather than going out to play, but this deliberation alone will never conclude with you representing work as attractive. It might lead you to represent work as something there is *reason* for you to do, and thereby to set work as an end—but then you will be working *in spite of not being attracted to it.* To get yourself to find work attractive, you will need to condition yourself, or get someone to condition you. Thus, according to the principle that *Normative Governance Requires Deliberative Responsiveness*, attraction is not the kind of mental state

---

43 We may of course demand rational justification for the failure to cultivate useful subrational attractions.

fundamentally governed by rational norms. That is to say, the deliberative *non-responsiveness* of attraction is a sign of a deeper conceptual truth about attraction: it is not a reason-based attitude.

However, subrational attractions can play an important role in rational motivation, because we often treat the fact that we are attracted to something as sufficient reason to pursue it. The result is a maxim based on subrational attraction—as Henry Allison says, we *incorporate* our attractions into maxims in order to act on them.[44] Several philosophers of Humean bent have argued that this theory of human action makes deliberation and choice unrealistically reflective. They see the Kantian as committed to the "foregrounding" of desire (they do not distinguish between attraction/inclination and rational end-setting) in deliberation. Consider how Simon Blackburn describes the Kantian account of the relation between desire and deliberation. He suggests the account and similar views treat the deliberating agent as the captain of a ship, and her desires as her crew:

> On these accounts, deliberation is essentially a matter of surveying (perhaps cursing and flogging) the crew from the quarter-deck. But this is wrong. The deliberative stance is actually one of surveying the surroundings— the situation of choice and the salient features. And this survey is done in the light of our concerns, represented by the crew. Deliberation is an active engagement with the *world*, not a process of introspecting our own consciousness of it. The last thing you want to do when you are wondering when to make your dash through the traffic, or whether to move bishop to rook 5, is to take your mind off the traffic or the chessboard.[45]

This depiction does indeed make the Kantian seem ridiculous. But it is a caricature. Blackburn pictures the Kantian deliberating agent as focused primarily, even exclusively, on her desires, losing her connection with the features of the world toward which her desires are directed. This agent, he suggests, doesn't deliberate about which restaurant has the best food, but about whether to satisfy her desire for the best food. And this is, in a certain sense, true—but Blackburn exaggerates the point. The Kantian point is that we *can* reflect on our attractions, we *can* consider whether our attraction to the best food is a good basis for choice, so when we *do* act in service of our attractions, we thereby are accountable for treating them as legitimate bases for action. This is true both descriptively and normatively. Descriptively, the person who acts on the basis of her attractions, by contrast with the person who is passively moved by her attractions, is disposed to appeal to her attractions in defense of her decision. Normatively, she is accountable for treating

---

44   Henry Allison, *Kant's Theory of Freedom.*
45   Simon Blackburn, *Ruling Passions: A Theory of Practical Reason* (Oxford: Oxford University Press, 1998), 254.

her attractions as justification for her decision, by contrast with the person who is passively moved and is instead accountable for failing to build up the strength of will to resist her attractions, or failing to work to change her attractions through nonrational means. (This is what I meant earlier when I said that, on the Kantian theory, we can give our subrational attractions "normative authority" by deciding to act on them.) Perhaps one shouldn't choose a restaurant exclusively on the basis of whether it has the best food—perhaps one also ought to take into account cost, or employment practices, or atmosphere. That is to say, perhaps the fact that one is attracted to the best food isn't a sufficient reason for action.

If an agent chooses a restaurant because it has the best food, this feature is most likely the justification she will offer if asked. This feature is not, however, by itself a complete justificatory rationale for her choice. As far as the considerations that she takes into direct account are concerned, her attraction to the best food probably functions in the background; but this attraction also implicitly enters into deliberation as justification for choosing on the basis of this feature. Her full rationale incorporates this feature *and the fact that it attracts her.* (Indeed, her full rationale most likely incorporates several other considerations, at least implicitly. If she would not choose the restaurant with the best food if it had miserable employment practices, then the absence of the latter feature is also part of her rationale.) In short, attractions can *provide* reasons, and therefore constitute justificatory rationales for action, but attractions are not themselves based on reasons—they are not the sorts of thing for which one has, or should have, a justificatory rationale.[46]

Hope as Incorporation

Standing ready to justify the thoughts, feelings, and plans I discussed in chapter 1, then, goes beyond being attracted to those activities or their consequences. It is a matter of adopting the end of engaging in those activities, treating one's attraction to the hoped-for outcome as a reason to engage in them. More precisely, it is being ready to appeal to that attraction, the hoped-for outcome's attractive features, and the licensing status of the outcome's probability as a sufficient justificatory rationale for what one does. This is what makes hope a distinctive attitude: the hopeful person treats this set of considerations as a sufficient justificatory rationale for engaging in the these activities. A crucial element of this rationale is the hoped-for outcome's probability. As the hopeful person sees it, this probability permits

---

46 That is, a direct justificatory rationale; one may have, and probably sometimes is accountable for having, a justificatory rationale for adopting courses of action that results in one having certain attractions.

other considerations to provide reasons for engaging in those activities. She thereby *incorporates* her attraction into her rational agency in a way that the despairing person resists. That is why I call this the "incorporation" analysis of hope.

So far, I have argued that to hope for an outcome is to:

1 Be attracted to the outcome in virtue of certain of its features;
2 Assign a probability between and exclusive of 0 and 1 to the outcome;
3 Adopt a stance toward that probability whereby it licenses treating one's attraction to the outcome (and the outcome's attractive features) as a reason for certain ways of thinking, feeling, and/or planning with regard to the hoped-for outcome; and
4 Treat one's attraction and the outcome's attractive features as sufficient reason for those ways of thinking, feeling, and/or planning.

As I discussed in the introduction, this analysis should not be read as providing a set of necessary and sufficient conditions for hope. In particular, many of the elements are not *necessary* for hope. Though we might want to say that hope *in the fullest sense* involves all of them, it remains plausible that we should attribute hope to some individuals who do not fully incorporate their attractions and probability estimates in all of the ways described. As an account of hope in the fullest sense, this analysis makes sense of the differences in hope that we see in *Cancer Research, Shawshank Redemption,* and *Lottery Ticket*—while respecting the intuition that the characters could share the same desires and probability estimates.

Understanding the incorporation analysis as a syndrome account also tells us what we should say about situations where our feelings of anticipation and our fantasies are recalcitrant to our judgments. Sometimes, that is, we find ourselves indulging in hopeful fantasies, feelings, even plans, all while judging that the low probability of the desired outcome means we shouldn't. Here, although we may resist hope, we cannot help but engage in hopeful activities. The incorporation analysis tells us exactly why this is not full-fledged hope, but potentially worth calling "hope" anyway—enough of the elements of hope are present.

Under the incorporation analysis, hope emerges as an attitude governed by both theoretical and practical norms; it is bound to represent the world accurately, but also to support our rational agency—that is, to cohere with and contribute to our rational schemes of ends.[47] Because it involves a subjective probability estimate, hope is answerable to the evidence for the outcome's probability. This is an important aspect of hope and, as we will see in

---

47 On this conception of practical rationality, see the comparison with Rawls earlier in this chapter.

chapter 3, there are activities expressive of hope that can cause the hopeful person to ignore relevant evidence and overestimate the chances that her hope will be realized. This potential is of particular concern to people dealing with situations like *Cancer Research*, where standards for informed consent require that research participants genuinely comprehend the risks and benefits of their participation. If by fantasizing about a cure or indulging her feelings of anticipation, a person like Bess comes to irrationally adjust her probability assignment, then she runs the risk of undermining her own informed consent. I do think, however, that much of the clinical literature on hope misunderstands the nature of this particular danger. A number of articles and studies suggest it is irrational to hope *at all* when one's chances are extremely slim.[48] Yet, if the incorporation analysis is right, this is to misunderstand the structure of hope. One can simultaneously assign a rational probability estimate, even an extremely low one, to an outcome and see that probability as licensing a powerful hope—that is, a great deal of mental, emotional, and physical activity focused on the outcome. As long as this activity promotes one's rational ends and does not cause one to irrationally adjust one's probability assignment, this powerful hope is rational. To return to Alan and Bess, the cancer research participants: their hopes are different not because they desire a cure to different degrees or assign different probability estimates to a cure, but because they incorporate these attitudes into their rational schemes of ends differently. Alan invests less in the possibility of a cure: he thinks the slim chance of benefitting from his trial participation licenses only a small amount of positive feeling, thought, and planning centered on a cure. Bess, by contrast, sees the same slim chance as licensing a *great deal* of such investment. The point that now emerges is that *they may both be fully rational*. If Bess's rational scheme of ends coheres with, or even benefits from, such investment—perhaps she *needs* such a strong investment to keep her scheme from falling apart, and if this is so, then her hope is rational. And perhaps Alan's rational scheme of ends does not thus cohere or benefit. Perhaps *he* needs to dedicate greater energy to preparing for his death to keep his scheme from falling apart; and if so, his hope is rational.

Of course, this practical side of hope poses its own risks. Just as some hopeful activities can cause epistemic irrationality, they can contribute to practical irrationality. In particular, certain ways of fantasizing about a hoped-for outcome can detract from one's ability to turn intention into action, and detract also from one's ability to form plans responsive to real-world obstacles. I discuss these hazards in the next chapter. Before turning to these matters,

---

48   For example, L. J. Schneiderman, "The Perils of Hope," *Cambridge Quarterly of Healthcare Ethics* 14.2 (Spring 2005): 235–39. Jerome Groopman's *The Anatomy of Hope: How People Prevail in the Face of Illness* (New York: Random House, 2004) is sometimes suggestive of this view, but I think it is ultimately more nuanced.

though, I want to make one final important point about the nature of hope under this analysis.

Hoping and End-Setting

I have argued that hoping for an outcome involves standing ready to offer a particular justificatory rationale for certain activities and feelings related to the outcome. And I have further suggested that "standing ready" to justify an activity or action should be understood as adopting an end—treating certain considerations as sufficient reason to engage in the activity. Thus hope is, in part, an exercise of rational agency; it is *active*. (It is also passive in part, because it involves being attracted to the outcome.)[49]

It is all too easy to slide from this observation of hope's active aspect to conceiving of hoping for an outcome as setting the end of *pursuing the hoped-for outcome*. Let's call this the "end-setting conception" of hope. In support of this conception is the fact that setting the end of bringing about the hoped-for outcome involves treating pursuit of the outcome as justified, and activities like fantasizing about the hoped-for outcome and feeling positive anticipation of it could be instrumental to this pursuit. These considerations could make sense of the fact that hope manifests as a syndrome of thoughts, feelings, and activities, while also accounting for the fact that the hopeful person stands ready to deploy justificatory concepts, unlike the person who is merely attracted to the same outcome.

Although neither explicitly endorses the end-setting conception of hope, both Margaret Urban Walker and Victoria McGeer write about hope in a way that is highly suggestive of this conception.[50] Walker describes hope as "An emotional stance or 'affective attitude,' a recognizable syndrome that is characterized by certain desires and perceptions, but also by certain forms of attention, expression, feeling, and activity."[51] The certain forms of attention, etc., are "perceptions, feelings, and dispositions to feel, think, and act in some ways that move the one who hopes *in the direction of having what is hoped*

---

49 "Adopting an end" is, as I have noted, subject to a dispositional analysis: being disposed to offer certain considerations in defense of one's decisions; so, although the incorporation analysis makes hope partially an active thing, it does not require that hope or its elements always rise to conscious awareness.

50 At times Alan Mittleman also seems to endorse the end-setting conception of hope. For example: "To hope requires not only the possibility of change but the possibility of action to effectuate change. Desire daydreams; hope issues in a course of action," *Hope in a Democratic Age* (Oxford: Oxford University Press, 2009), 2–3. Ultimately, however, the form of hope he most thoroughly endorses is more about preservation than effectuating change, and more an evaluative orientation than a concrete commitment to action (see especially the concluding chapter of the book, 258–70).

51 Walker, *Moral Repair*, 48.

for come about.[52] McGeer writes in similar terms, emphasizing the idea that hope involves a certain kind of "agential investment."[53] Walker and McGeer cite each other approvingly, so I will take their conceptions of hope as variants of the same view. Let me say a bit more about why I think their view is at least suggestive of the end-setting conception of hope.

McGeer's and Walker's view is that in order to truly count as hoping for an outcome, one has to invest some of one's agency in it. Although they tend to talk about hope as a "force" or "energy," it is clear they think of invested agency as a matter of dispositions to display certain patterns in one's thoughts, feelings, and actions. Now, as I argued earlier, even subrational attraction—in a sense the most passive form of motivation of which we are capable—involves such dispositions. What, then, is hope, that it goes beyond attraction? Walker writes:

> In hoping, we become alert to the ways and means by which the hoped for circumstance could come about. We imagine scenarios in which what is hoped for comes to pass and plays out before us. We create ideas and plans and awaken anticipation, excitement, or pleasure about what its realization and consequences will be like.[54]

As before, this remark doesn't pin down how exactly hope is supposed to surpass attraction. Indeed Walker's description coheres relatively nicely with the incorporation analysis—so one possibility is that we are in complete agreement about how best to conceive of hope. However, the focus on the awareness of "ways and means" can also be interpreted as suggestive of setting the hoped-for outcome as an end. When we set an end, we treat it or some of its features as providing us with sufficient reason to commit ourselves to taking the means to achieving it, and to seeking out or creating means when none are perceived. This commitment usually takes the form of a plan, which may be merely schematic, though it also may be very detailed. We then fit this plan together with our other plans, adjusting where and when necessary.[55] The key difference between being attracted to an outcome and setting the end of bringing it about, that is, lies in one's relation to "ways and means." Being attracted to an outcome does not require caring about or thinking about means to realizing it—it is possible to be attracted in a fully passive way. Once we enter the realm of strategizing and planning, and of treating a possible outcome as providing reason to pursue it, we are in the

52 Ibid., 50 (emphasis added)
53 Victoria McGeer, "The Art of Good Hope," *Annals of the American Academy of Political and Social Sciences* 592 (2004): 100–27; and Victoria McGeer, "Trust, Hope and Empowerment," *Australasian Journal of Philosophy* 86.2 (2008): 237–54.
54 Walker, *Moral Repair*, 50.
55 Michael Bratman, *Intentions, Plans, and Practical Reason* (Cambridge, MA: Harvard University Press, 1987).

realm of end-setting. Thus, one plausible spin on McGeer's and Walker's view is that hoping means setting the end of realizing the hoped-for outcome.

This is a tempting idea, but I think it is mistaken. Although hoping for an outcome does involve setting certain ends—namely the ends of engaging in the activities discussed in the previous chapter—it does not necessarily involve setting the end of *bringing about the hoped-for outcome*. That is, hope does involve rational desires, but not necessarily the rational desire for the hoped-for outcome. To see this, we need another set of cases.

Cases: Hoping without End-Setting

There are two kinds of counterexamples to the end-setting conception of hope. First, there are cases of hoping for an outcome one knows one has no chance of influencing, such as the hope for good weather for one's picnic tomorrow, the hope that a long-lost relative is flourishing, or the hope that Hitler was miserable when he died.[56] Second, there are cases of hoping for an outcome one has taken no steps to influence, and intends to take no steps to influence. For example, I usually have pretty strong hopes regarding which candidate the Republican party nominates to run for president—I hope they choose the weakest candidate, or the candidate who will be least destructive if he or she ends up winning the office (or I am torn between these two hopes). But I never make any effort to influence the nomination process: I don't give money to the candidate I pin my hopes on, nor do I talk him or her up to Republicans I know, or anything like that.

To be clear, these cases are not necessarily trivial, or examples of what Pettit calls "the lowest common denominator" of hope. All of these examples could be profoundly important hopes that seriously occupy the people entertaining them. The picnic tomorrow could be one's last chance to romance the person for whom one is sick with love; one could have a beloved family member who struggles with life-threatening depression after surviving the Holocaust. And when I anticipate a tight presidential race, it really matters a lot to me who gets the Republican nomination. So a person might have these hopes in a robust way even while she acknowledges that the outcomes are beyond her power to influence, and, moreover, she has no intention of exercising the power she does have.[57]

---

56 Thanks to Jeppe von Platz for the Hitler example.

57 Let me also mention a third, more esoteric counterexample to the end-setting conception of hope, which I call "unimaginable" hope. Unimaginable hope is hope for an outcome that outstrips the hopeful person's conceptual resources. If unimaginable hope is genuine hope—and I think it is, though I do not think it is necessarily *more* genuine or otherwise superior to hopes that stay within our concepts—then it is difficult to see how the end-setting conception can be

The End-Setting Conception's Inability to Accommodate These Cases

The advocates of the end-setting conception may respond to these counter-examples in a few ways. One way is to dismiss or deflate them. When we talk about hopes regarding past events, Walker says, we "borrow on the *futurity* of hope—hope goes to what hovers before us with a sense that all is not decided *for us*; what is not yet known is 'as if' open to . . . action, for all one knows."[58] Similarly, McGeer argues:

> [H]ope in the limit case [i.e., the case where the hoped-for outcome is closed to influence] is still about taking an agential interest in the future and the opportunities it may afford. It is about saying the following: although there may be nothing we can do now to bring about what we desire, our energy is still oriented toward the future, limitations notwithstanding. . . . [W]e lean into the future ready to act when action can do some good.[59]

Strictly speaking, what McGeer and Walker say here is false. In hoping for Hitler's misery one does not see the question as "open to action," and one does not "lean into the future." It is *over and done* and there is nothing anyone can do to make it more likely. But of course this is not precisely what they mean. I take it they are claiming we implicitly perceive an analogy between the kind of uncertainty at play in the cases where what we hope for *is* open to action and the kind of uncertainty at play in cases where we form desires about an unknown past. On the basis of this analogy, we extend the concept of hope from the first kind of case to the second. "I hope for [a past outcome]" is semantically parasitic on "I hope for [an outcome open to my influence]."

This is an interesting claim. It is also a strong claim, in that it makes an entire class of our apparent hopes not "real" hopes, but imitations or echoes of another. I see no reason to accept this claim rather than the claim that hope entails uncertainty about the hoped-for outcome, and that uncertainty could be a recognition of any of the hopeful person's epistemic and/or agential limits—e.g., her lack of knowledge regarding the past, present or future;

---

right. For how can we include among our ends that which we cannot even conceive. Unimaginable hopes are the subject of chapter 4. They are also rather esoteric, so I do not want my case against the end-setting conception to turn on them. Therefore, in what follows, I will rely solely on the first two counterexamples of hoping for an outcome one knows one has no chance of influencing and hoping for an outcome one has no intention of trying to influence. I believe these cases are all we need to see that the end-setting conception of hope is mistaken.

58 Walker, *Moral Repair*, 45. The complete passage says that "what is not yet known is 'as if' open to *chance and* action."

59 McGeer, "The Art of Good Hope," 104.

her inability to predict the outcomes of chance; her inability to guarantee the outcome happens; and so on.

The agential investment view therefore requires the positive argument that hopes for outcomes perceived as open to agential influence are more "genuine" or fundamental than others. Indeed, it needs a more ambitious argument, given cases like my hope for a certain outcome of the Republican nominations—that is, cases where the seemingly hopeful person perceives the outcome as open to action, but does not set the outcome as an end. Walker argues that these cases are also not genuine hopes, but rather wishful thinking. She writes:

> In part, this is a conceptual point, a point about what we take hoping to be. We mark the difference between wishing and hoping precisely by noting whether individuals work to sustain and augment the feelings that will carry them through to some course of action.[60]

However, the difference between hoping and engaging in wishful thinking does not help exclude our cases from the category of genuine hopes. Generally speaking, when we pejoratively call an attitude "wishful thinking," we are saying both that it aims at something highly unlikely or impossible and that the wishful person is lost in flights of fancy. And neither of these claims is true, for example, about my hope regarding the Republican nominee. I believe the chances are good that the person I hope receives the nomination will, and I have no thoughts about fanciful influences or even remarkable coincidences producing this result. If I thought the only way this person would win would be if large numbers of New Hampshire voters didn't show up at the polls, and I therefore performed a voodoo ritual to make these voters sick or simply fantasized about a sudden widespread attack of a debilitating flu, *then* I would call this wishful thinking. But that is not the case, and I therefore see no reason to think my hope is not a genuine hope.

We have not seen a good reason to consider hopes for past events (like Hitler's misery), for present future events beyond one's influence (like a long-lost loved one's flourishing, or the weather), or for outcomes one has no intention of trying to influence (like the Republicans' choice of a nominee) as anything less than genuine hopes. Thus the end-setting conception of hope needs a way to treat these hopes as genuine. But seemingly the best it can do is say that, when we entertain such hopes, we are *disposed* to adopt the relevant ends—if the Hitler hater were to acquire control over the past, he would try to ensure Hitler's misery; if the picnic planner came to believe in a sun dance's efficacy, she would dance. At this point, however, we've lost sight of the difference between being attracted to an outcome and setting the end of bringing it about. Being subrationally attracted to an outcome does dispose

60 Walker, *Moral Repair*, 153.

one to set the end of trying to bring it about—though it certainly does not determine one to do so. In short, in trying to account for these counterexamples, the end-setting conception elides the distinction between subrational attraction and rational end-setting. And so the conception collapses back into the orthodox definition, with its inability to account for cases of hoping against hope.

Conclusion: A Unified Theory of Hope and the Worry about Excessive Reflectiveness

According to the incorporation analysis, hope constitutes, in addition to an attraction to the hoped-for outcome and a probability assignment between 0 and 1 to that outcome, standing ready to offer a certain justificatory rationale for certain activities related to the outcome. These hopeful activities are: turning one's attention and thoughts—especially by constructing fantasies—to the outcome; feeling a positive sense of anticipation—feeling "hopeful"—about it; and relying on it in one's plans—though only with a back-up plan. The justificatory rationale includes appealing to the probability one assigns to the outcome, as "good enough" to license these activities, along with treating one's attraction and the outcome's attractive features as reasons to engage in them. At the same time, the hopeful person does not necessarily treat any features of the hoped-for outcome as reasons to try to bring it about.

Hope is thus a distinctive way of exercising one's rational agency. It is a way of making an attractive outcome a part of one's mental, emotional, and planning activities, without setting out to bring it about. This is why I say hope is a distinctive way of incorporating one's attraction to an outcome into one's agency.

In developing and defending the incorporation analysis of hope, I have focused on cases of "hoping against hope." One might think, as a result of this focus, that this analysis does not apply to more prosaic, everyday hopes. More, one might find it implausible to think that, when we hope to find a good parking place, hope our friend caught the train on time, hope it does not rain on our picnic, and so on, the full apparatus of the incorporation analysis is in play. Thus one might think the orthodox definition is a sufficient account of prosaic hope, while something like the incorporation analysis is needed to fully characterize the special category of hopes held "against hope."

I think, though, that this would be a mistaken conclusion to draw at this point, and that cases of hoping against hope are just cases where the full nature of hope *in general* is most salient. The incorporation analysis should be seen, I believe, as providing a *unified* theory of hope in general: prosaic and profound. Why think this? I offer two lines of thought in support.

First, on the idea of "the full apparatus of the incorporation analysis." Once we recognize the incorporation element of hope, we need a lot of words, many of them fairly technical, to provide a precise characterization of the attitude. It is easy enough to infer from this fact that hope so characterized is itself complicated and technical—and so it is easy enough to think that this cannot be an accurate characterization of prosaic hope, which seems so simple and non-technical. But we should not conflate *familiar* phenomena or experiences with conceptually simple ones. The components of the incorporation element of hope are in fact very ordinary and familiar. In particular, we humans are constantly engaged in inter- and intra-personal justification; our default position with regard to everything we do, feel, and think is that we do, feel, and think it *for reasons*. As I have emphasized, this does not mean we always or even often explicitly articulate these reasons, but we are usually disposed to offer them in support of the things we do, feel, and think, and we generally think we and others *should* be able to offer them. This mode of being in the world is so standard that we do not usually need a philosophically precise characterization of it to recognize or unreflectively understand what we are doing. So the mere fact that prosaic hope seems so ordinary and familiar should not encourage us to think it does not involve justificatory elements like the licensing stance and rational desires. Indeed, the fact that our ordinary and familiar experience is shot through with both dispositions to inter- and intra-personal justification and the presupposition that we are normatively on the hook for such justifications *supports* thinking of "prosaic" phenomena in terms like these.

Second, consider what it would mean if the incorporation analysis did *not* extend to a prosaic hope like the hope that one's friend caught the train on time. It would become very difficult to conceptually parse this hope from an equally prosaic "despair" regarding this outcome. In other words, the arguments of chapter 1 can be run on prosaic attitudes as much as profound ones. Now, what makes a hope prosaic is usually that it regards an outcome one is not terribly invested in, and thus the feelings, thoughts, and/or plans one dedicates toward the outcome are not likely to have powerful occurrent presences. Similarly, the incorporation element, whereby one is committed to a certain sort of justification for these feelings, thoughts, and/or plans, is liable to stay at the level of unactualized disposition—no one is likely to demand one's rationale, including oneself. But without these elements, we are stuck with something like the orthodox definition, which is as consistent with prosaic despair as hope.

Finally, we should return to the worry previously alluded to, that the incorporation analysis makes hope into too reflective or sophisticated a phenomenon. The fact that this analysis can be understood in dispositional and normative terms, rather than requiring the attribution of explicit or occurrent mental states, should alleviate concerns about its applicability to mundane and "quiet" hopes. Nevertheless, some readers might still be troubled by the analysis's implication that creatures without robust concepts of reasons or justification are incapable of hope: even highly intelligent and social nonhuman animals and very young human children cannot be described accurately by the incorporation analysis. Can it really be right that these creatures are not capable of hope?

I think it is right, and that we should not be troubled, because these creatures *are* capable of something very like hope, an attitude that is developmentally continuous with the hope captured by the incorporation analysis. It's especially helpful here to think about children. As early as age three, children begin engaging in quasi- or proto-justifying behavior: they counter denials of their desires by declaring, "But I want it!" and they protest the "unfairness" of others' actions. Even if they do not have the full-blown concept of a justifying reason, they are well on their way, entertaining the possibility that their desires (attractions) make a claim on themselves and others and are worth appealing to in a justificatory manner. And so they are well on their way to full-blown hope, even if they are not quite there yet. Highly intelligent and social nonhuman animals are likely at some slightly earlier stage than children on the developmental scale. Some even have the capacity to plan and daydream, and some even a reflective awareness of their own beliefs and desires (though of course all of the claims in this paragraph are matters for empirical investigation), and they thus have the capacity for something very like hope.

We now have a complete account of hope conceived under the incorporation analysis. In the next two chapters, I turn to questions regarding the relationship between hope and motivation: is hope a distinctive form of motivation? Is it a *specially powered* form of motivation that equips us to do battle in the direst circumstances? Is it our best or only defense against despair, in such circumstances? I begin, in chapter 3, by arguing that, while hope in general can indeed influence motivation in unique ways, it is not itself a special form of motivation, and it is as capable of undermining motivation as it is of strengthening it. I then turn, in chapter 4, to a distinctive form of hope, which is best understood, I argue, as *faith*.

Suicide and Sustenance

Virtue and Sustenance

The idea that hope is a virtue traces most likely to St. Paul, who included it among the three Christian theological virtues: hope, faith, and charity.[1] Adopting this taxonomy, Aquinas argued that, although hope takes many different objects, it always relies on God as the efficient cause of its object, because we hope only for that which we conceive as good and God is the source of all goodness.[2] All hope, as long as it does not mistakenly take something bad as its object, is thus virtuous. Despite these roots, acceptance of the claim that hope is a virtue extends far beyond the reach of Christian doctrine. This is, no doubt, due to the widely held belief that hope has a special sustaining power. It is seen as that which sustains us through wartime, death camps, slavery, natural disaster, extreme disease and disability—a light, a beacon, the last spark that fuels us when all else has failed. In this chapter, I aim to determine in what sense, if any, this widely held belief is true. In chapter 5, I return to religious hope.

Let's begin by unpacking this claim: "Hope has a unique sustaining power in the context of a trial." First, a "trial" is a significant threat to one's ability to live well, to thrive or flourish.[3] What is it to "live well"? The answer I want here is not one that presupposes a worked-out virtue theory, since I am interested in examining what support the incorporation analysis of hope might lend to the popular view that hope is a virtue because of its special sustaining power. Pre-theoretically, then, "living well" is largely a subjective matter, but with objective constraints. That is, the possible ways of living well vary widely from person to person, depending on what the individual cares about; but there are limits: for example, a life dedicated to immoral action or

---

1 The idea that hope is *connected to* virtue is at least as old as Aristotle, who held that certain forms of hope give rise to the virtue of courage, and provide the motive to deliberation, which is necessary for the exercise of any virtue. See G. Scott Gravlee, "Aristotle on Hope," *Journal of the History of Philosophy* 38.4 (2000): 461–77.

2 Aquinas, *Summa Theologiae*, 2a 2ae Q17 A4.

3 I borrow the term "trial" from Gabriel Marcel, whose view I discuss later in the chapter.

to the complete squandering of all of one's natural talents cannot be the life of a person who "lives well."[4]

Second, to say hope has a "sustaining power" in the context of a trial is not necessarily to say hope helps one *overcome* the trial, or bring the trial to an end. Sometimes, when people talk about hope sustaining them, they mean it helps them work within the constraints imposed by the trial. Through hope, they find a new way of living well in spite of the trial. It is possible that this discovery brings an end to the trial, in the sense that the unchanged circumstances no longer constitute a trial. More likely, the hopeful person continues to find disease, disability, depression, imprisonment, loss of a loved one, creative stagnancy, unemployment, or what-have-you a significant restriction on her ability to live well; but hope helps her find a way to live well enough that she finds her situation tolerable and does not suffer agony. Such a hope qualifies as a "sustaining" hope. This is why I think the popular belief that hope has sustaining power is connected with the idea that hope is a virtue. Life presents us with trials, and living well requires coping with them. If hope helps one find a way to live well by either overcoming or living within the constraints of her trial, then in this sense it is a virtue.

We should also observe that, insofar as the common view of hope as sustenance relies on the notion that hope is incompatible with willing one's own destruction—or ceasing to will one's continued existence—it is mistaken. Suicide is in fact often an act of hope. This claim may strike some as counterintuitive. There are those who seem to agree with Philippa Foot when she writes, "Except in certain fairly rare cases . . . suicide is contrary to the virtue of hope."[5] Now, Foot may mean simply that there are *forms* of hope that sustain us through our trials (and are therefore virtuous), and that suicide is contrary to *these*. If that is her meaning then what she says is practically a tautology—and what I am trying to do here is identify the forms of hope. However, she goes on to say that hope is "of course" a virtue because of the way it counteracts the belief that "all is lost," and she does not qualify this to allow that there could be hopes or ways of hoping that are not virtuous; this suggests she thinks suicide is essentially an anti-hopeful act. By this reasoning, many might object to my claim: surely suicide is an act of *despair*; surely suicide is what people do when they have given up all hope?[6]

4 Perhaps squandering all of one's natural talents is immoral. I don't intend these examples as mutually exclusive or even jointly exhaustive ways of failing to live well.

5 Philippa Foot, *Natural Goodness* (Oxford: Clarendon Press, 2001), 74n.

6 Mittleman argues that we can tell hope is a virtue precisely because it is opposed to despair (Mittleman, 58). However, he also explicitly recognizes that there are non-virtuous forms of hope. As I will argue in chapter 4, I disagree with Mittleman regarding what forms of hope are virtuous in the sense that they are essentially opposed to despair—he believes secular hope is ultimately

Having read first-person accounts of depression and talked with people suffering extreme trials, I am convinced that, while there is also a sense in which suicide can be an act of despair, it is not necessarily what people do when they give up *all* hope—it can instead be what they do when the idea of death promises, to their eyes, the only possible end to their unendurable trial. Through suicide, they hope to escape. It is certainly the case that many people are most in danger of succumbing to their trial," when the idea of death is accompanied with a feeling of relief, or with the hopeful feeling of anticipation discussed in chapter 1. When they commit suicide, it is an act of despair only in the sense that they have despaired of any other way of coping with their trial. It is an act of hope in the sense that it presupposes a hopeful view of death.[7]

A caveat: I am not saying suicide is *never* a virtuous response to a trial. Sometimes, imminent death is inevitable, and suicide is the only way to die well. I also believe suicide can be a virtuous response to imminent agony, extreme loss of function, or the betrayal of one's values (as when one knows one will not be able to withstand torture). Nor am I saying the hope one might receive from the possibility of suicide could *never* sustain one through a trial. It is possible that, by keeping before one's mind this possibility in a hopeful way, one might find the courage to endure things one should endure but otherwise could not. Something like this seems to be at work in Jim Witcher's experience of rapidly progressing ALS, depicted in the PBS miniseries *On Our Own Terms: Moyers on Dying*. Witcher first copes with his disease by declaring that he wants to end his life when he can no longer feed himself; when he reaches that point, he says he wants to end his life when he can no longer swallow; and on it goes—at each loss of capacity, he finds a way to live, seemingly in part by holding out the prospect of suicide at the next loss.[8] Similarly, statistics from Oregon, where physician-assisted suicide is an option for certain terminally ill people, show that many people prepare the way for suicide but then never exercise the option—simply having the option available appears to contribute to their ability to die well.[9]

---

unable to function in this way, but I will argue that there is a form of secular hope that has the same sustaining structure as religious faith.

7   In my discussion of Marcel, in chapter 4, I will grant that it makes sense to call seeing suicide in a hopeful way, given certain qualifications, "existential despair."

8   Witcher's experience is complex. He does not "cope" with his loss of capacity with quick equanimity; he is angry and grief-stricken for much of the documentary. A good deal of his anger is directed at the fact that his state, Louisiana, does not allow physician-assisted suicide, and so he must plan suicide through an overdose of the drugs he has access to as a veterinarian. Nevertheless, it is striking how at each stage of his illness the prospect of suicide remains before his mind and yet gets pushed forward to the next loss of capacity.

9   The annual reports are available at: http://public.health.oregon.gov/ProviderPartnerResources/EvaluationResearch/DeathwithDignityAct/Pages/index.aspx.

So, sometimes the hope provided by suicide may qualify as a sustaining hope, either because it leads to suicide and suicide is genuinely the best way to bring one's trial to an end, or because it helps one live well enough within the confines of the trial. It is clear, however, that sometimes the prospect of suicide is the source of a dangerous hope—a hope that makes it more likely that a person who could indeed live reasonably well through certain efforts will instead end her life. In such cases, it is simply not true that any hope is better than none. In such cases, a person needs something to sustain her, and hope instead destroys her.

Thus we ought to qualify the view that hope has a unique power to sustain us through trials, even while we seek a way in which this might be true. The idea is not that *just any* hope has this power, or that hope can never be destructive. What we want to know is what hope has to be like if it is to have this power. Does it have to have a particular object? Does it have to have a particular source? Does it have to play out in particular ways? I take a Goldilocks approach to answering these questions, examining and rejecting two extremes before settling on a view somewhere in the middle.

The First Extreme: Aquinas and Irascible Hope

Even given the above qualifications as regards sustenance, it is tempting to think hope can sustain us through trials only if it is a special kind of super-charged motive force, capable of barreling through all barriers. Indeed, it is this thought that leads many of the opponents of the orthodox definition to their opposition. For, on this definition, the only motivational force at work in hope is desire, which seems too prosaic to power us through profound obstacles. And one might be suspicious of the incorporation analysis for the same reason: the motivational powers at work in hope are the same ones at work in all exercises of rational agency; hope is not a unique power.

Quite independently of his arguments that hope is a theological virtue, Aquinas argues that hope must be an "irascible appetite," because otherwise it would be unable to power us through obstacles to the achievement of our desires.[10] More broadly, he argues that we must have two distinct motivational powers—the "concupiscible" and the "irascible"—if we are to explain our ability to overcome obstacles; and hope, as one of our responses to obstacles, is an exercise of this power. I will argue that our ability to overcome obstacles presupposes only one motivational power, guided by belief in the existence of said obstacles. We do need two distinct motivational powers to explain the agent's experience of her own attractions and to give a full

---

10 Shade, in *Habits of Hope*, endorses Aquinas's view of hope as a form of motivation especially suited to overcoming "arduous" obstacles to goods.

account of hope, as discussed in the previous chapter. For the sake of evaluating Aquinas's position, however, it will be enough to focus on the presuppositions of our ability to overcome obstacles. So, for present purposes, I will be defending the explanatory power of a Humean or Lockean, monist theory of motivation.[11]

The Thomistic "Inner Cathedral"

Peter King offers an apt metaphor for Aquinas's faculty psychology. It is, he suggests, structured like a cathedral, in virtue of two intersecting distinctions between types of psychological powers: the appetitive versus the cognitive, and the sensitive versus the intellective.[12] Appetitive powers are responsible for movement, while cognitive powers are what allow us to receive and process information. Human beings share sensitive powers with nonhuman animals, but are unique among earthly creatures in possessing intellective powers—the former are responsible for the perception of concrete and particular objects, as well as for animal movement, while the latter are the seat of reason, responsible for knowledge of universals, and for rational volition (the will). Hence, we have four psychological capacities: sensitive cognition, sensitive appetite, intellectual cognition, and intellectual appetite. Aquinas argues that the passions, including hope, belong to the sensitive appetite. First, the fact that they motivate indicates they are appetitive and not cognitive:

> [T]he word "passion" implies that the patient is drawn to that which belongs to the agent. Now the soul is drawn to a thing by the appetitive power rather than by the apprehensive [i.e. cognitive] power: because the soul has, through its appetitive power, an order to things as they are in themselves.[13]

Passions are, as their name indicates, passive, insofar as when one undergoes a passion one is being acted upon. But they also move us. As Aquinas notes, passions draw us toward their object (when their object is good or beneficial; they repel us away from objects cognized as evil or harmful). Hence they must be appetitive, because the cognitive faculties move us only by influencing the appetitive in virtue of representing objects as good or evil.

11 I hasten to add that the monist theory of motivation is Humean, and not necessarily Hume's. I actually think the dominant, "Humean" view of these matters diverges from Hume's in fairly significant ways.

12 Peter King, "The Inner Cathedral: Mental Architecture in High Scholasticism," *Vivariu* 46 (2008): 253–74.

13 Aquinas, *Summa Theologiae*, 1a 2ae Q22 A2.

Second, a connection between the passions and bodily changes indicates that they are sensitive and not intellectual: "[P]assion is properly to be found where there is corporeal transmutation. This corporeal transmutation is found in the act of the sensitive appetite."[14] Aquinas holds that, though the passions are occurrent psychological states with intentional objects, they are also essentially physical. Anger, for example, essentially involves "a kindling of the blood about the heart."[15] The intellectual powers, by contrast, are essentially immaterial (though they may have contingent or "accidental" connections to bodily changes).

The Concupiscible and Irascible Passions

Aquinas first distinguishes the concupiscible and irascible powers of the sensitive appetite in the First Part of the *Summa*, in the course of laying out the general architecture of his faculty psychology:

> [T]here must needs be in the sensitive part to appetitive powers—one through which the soul is simply inclined to seek what is suitable, according to the senses, and to fly from what is hurtful, and this is called the concupiscible: and another, whereby an animal resists these attacks that hinder what is suitable, and inflict harm, and this is called the irascible. Whence we say that its object is something arduous, because its tendency is to overcome and rise against obstacles.[16]

This need for two appetitive powers within the sensitive soul is supposed to be analogous to a need of "natural" things—i.e., plants, rocks, and other parts of the natural world that lack a sensitive soul. Aquinas argues that it is not enough for fire to tend to move upward; it also needs a tendency to deal with obstacles to this movement by, for example, dividing around a poker inserted in its way. Analogously, an animal needs not only an inclination to move toward a watering hole, but also an inclination to deal with obstacles by, say, confronting or evading a competitor for the resource.

So far, it seems the Humean who believes there is only one motivational power should have no trouble accommodating this distinction. The label "irascible," she says, designates desires that presuppose the use of instrumental reasoning: the animal represents the water as attractive or desirable and the act of evading the competitor as instrumental to drinking the water, and this generates a representation of evading the competitor as attractive, as well. But perhaps this is not all Aquinas means by the distinction.

---

14   Ibid., 1a 2ae Q22 A3.
15   Ibid., 1a 2ae Q22 A3 ad 3.
16   Ibid., 1a Q81 A2.

Powers are distinguished by their objects, according to Aquinas, and thus he goes on to distinguish the concupiscible and irascible powers:

[T]he object of the concupiscible power is sensible good or evil, simply apprehended as such, which causes pleasure or pain. But, since the soul must, of necessity, experience difficulty or struggle at times, in acquiring some such good, or in avoiding some such evil, insofar as such good or evil is more than our animal nature can easily acquire or avoid; therefore *this very good or evil, inasmuch as it is of an arduous or difficult nature,* is the object of the irascible faculty.[17]

There are six concupiscible passions and five irascible. The concupiscible are, as defined above, direct responses to good and evil as such: love and hatred for the present good and evil, desire and aversion for good and evil "not yet possessed," and joy and sorrow for good and evil not previously possessed but now present. The irascible passions arise from the concupiscible, when it is added that the good or evil is difficult to obtain or avoid, respectively. Here we find hope, despair, fear, daring, and anger. This characterization suggests the irascible passions are transformations of the concupiscible, which occur when the latter's object comes to be cognized as difficult to attain (if good) or difficult to avoid (if evil). Thus it will not do to reserve the label "irascible" for desires resulting from instrumental reasoning; the distinction between good or evil objects and those same objects under the aspect of difficulty is orthogonal to the distinction between instrumental and unmotivated attractions or desires.

Consider the following example from Susan James: "When . . . a student wants to stop working but knows she ought to continue, her concupiscible desire to stop may be resisted by her irascible appetite to the point where *ira*, strengthening her desire to continue, keeps her at her desk."[18] The student originally has a concupiscible desire to study, or to achieve some goal that requires studying (i.e., the desire to study might be either unmotivated or motivated), and this alone may be enough to move her to study, so long as she perceives no obstacles to doing so. As soon as she becomes bored or tired or distracted, however, she cognizes the activity in a new way. Before, studying was just good or beneficial; now, it is a good made difficult to attain by the obstacle of her boredom. So now her concupiscible desire to study is transformed into the irascible passion of daring or determination to study. And now her concupiscible power is opposed to studying, but it is embattled by the irascible power's determination, which may win out in the end.

17 Ibid., 1a 2ae Q 23 A 1 (emphasis added).
18 Susan James, *Passion and Action: The Emotions in Seventeenth-Century Philosophy* (Oxford: Oxford University Press, 1997), 58.

Still, however, it seems the Humean should have no trouble accommodating the difference. Now she simply reserves the label "irascible" exactly as Aquinas says: it is used to designate desire for objects cognized as good but requiring effort and/or good fortune to attain (and aversions to objects that are cognized as evil but also as requiring effort and/or good fortune to avoid). But these are differences in how the object is cognized, not in the fundamental nature of the dispositions constituting the motivation.

Peter King thinks there is yet more to the irascible passions, such that the Humean (or as he calls it, the Lockean) account of motivation cannot accommodate them. His argument centers on a story about Jones, the man, teasing Rover the dog with a bone. Originally, Rover just desires the bone, but he quickly comes to see Jones as an obstacle to the bone, and thus becomes angry with him. Eventually, Rover may attack Jones out of this anger, even if Jones finally hands him the bone. King argues:

> [N]o matter what explanation the Lockean theory adopts, there is a basic question unanswered and indeed unaddressed. What prompts Rover to adopt the desire to attack Jones at all? Jones is not edible, as the bone is. Jones is not a natural target of canine aggression. Why does Rover attack Jones rather than merely circumventing him as quickly as possible? The answer is familiar from experience. Rover attacks Jones because Jones is a present evil, a threat to Rover's pursuit of pleasure, an obstacle to be overcome. But that is precisely to allow Aquinas's point that obstacles or difficulties themselves can be objects of passion. Furthermore, they are certainly not desire on a par with the simple push-pull model.[19]

Now, as noted before, the Humean (or Lockean) should have no trouble saying that Rover, through instrumental reasoning, develops a desire to eliminate an obstacle to acquiring the desired bone—thus, as long as Rover perceives Jones as such an obstacle, and perceives attacking him as a way of getting the bone, there really is no puzzle at all about how the desire to attack Jones arises. I take it the puzzle is supposed to be about how this desire acquires a life of its own, so to speak. Supposing Jones hands over the bone, why would Rover continue to be angry with him, if his anger is just a specific kind of instrumental desire?[20]

19   Peter King, "Aquinas on the Passions," 14.
20   Dogs are capable of instrumental reasoning. Instrumental reasoning does not require the capacity to employ the concept of a justificatory reason. Instrumental reasoning requires only the capacity to represent something as an instrument to an object that one represents *either* as attractive or as reason-providing. Thus my dog engages in instrumental reasoning when she either roots through my pocket or sits quietly as a way of getting the cheese she suspects is in my pocket—she represents the imagined cheese as *to-be-eaten*, and represents either theft or sitting quietly as *a way of getting the cheese*, and this pair of representations motivates her. I may engage in this very same

Of course, I am not at all committed to the notion that any emotional attitudes are subject to analysis in Humean terms. As I have argued, hope involves commitments of a rational nature, and I have argued elsewhere that love does, as well.[21] My concern here is simply to show that Aquinas has not identified a form of motivation that cannot be characterized accurately in terms of Humean attraction or desire and cognitive or doxastic circumstances. King thinks he has: namely, passions directed at obstacles to our desires that are capable of taking on lives of their own.

To emphasize, there is nothing mysterious, from a Humean perspective, about passions directed at obstacles to our desires. Here is Aquinas's careful breakdown of how this works:

> As we have often stated (22, 2; 35, 1; 41, 1), all these passions belong to the appetitive power. Now every movement of the appetitive power is reducible to one either of pursuit or of avoidance. Again, pursuit or avoidance is of something either by reason of itself or by reason of something else. By reason of itself, good is the object of pursuit, and evil, the object of avoidance: but by reason of something else, evil can be the object of pursuit, through some good attaching to it; and good can be the object of avoidance, through some evil attaching to it. Now that which is by reason of something else, follows that which is by reason of itself. Consequently pursuit of evil follows pursuit of good; and avoidance of good follows avoidance of evil.[22]

This is all consistent with a Humean account of motivation. We are attracted to or desire evil things insofar as we believe they are instrumental to good things; we have an aversion to good things insofar as we believe they lead to bad things. So the only question that remains is whether the Humean can account for passions originally directed at objects because of their instrumental value, which then linger in the absence of that value.

Or, really, the question that remains is whether the Humean can account for such passions *as well as* the Thomist can. Both Hume and Aquinas have an equal right to the observation that being passionate about an instrumentally good or evil object can lead one to discover other good or evil features of the object. Suppose one wants to climb Mt. Kilimanjaro. There are all sorts of instrumental desires one may form as a result—the desire to achieve a certain

---

form of instrumental reasoning, yet I may also engage in a form that involves the concept of a justificatory reason. So I may represent (my desire for) cheese as a sufficient reason to take the means to getting cheese, and represent a sequence of actions as a way of getting the cheese, and be motivated by this pair of representations. Thanks to Andrew Chignell for a conversation that prompted me to work out the place of instrumental reasoning in this picture.

21 Adrienne M. Martin, "Love and Agency," ms.

22 Aquinas, *Summa Theologiae*, 1a 2ae Q45 A2.

level of fitness, the desire to scrape together the money to travel to Africa, and so on. Inadequate fitness and a lack of funds are obstacles to achieving the original desire, and so improvements in these areas themselves become objects of desire. If they are cognized as requiring effort or good fortune to achieve, then they become the objects of an "irascible" passion. Once they cease to be cognized as instrumental to the original desired outcome—one learns that it is not as difficult to climb Mt. Kilimanjaro as one had thought, or that airfare to Africa is cheaper than one believed—they cease to be the objects of passions, concupiscible or irascible. This is true *unless* one has come to see some other good feature of improved fitness or finances, in which case one may continue to feel desire or other passions toward these objectives. One might, for example, come to see health as good in itself, and savings as helpful for achieving some other goal, and thus continue to be passionate about them.

The process just described could be what is going on with Rover's anger at Jones. This particular case of taunting could be the tipping point, where Rover comes to see Jones as a *general* source of pain, not just the source of this current pain. Jones thereby becomes an evil to be eliminated, because Rover cognizes him as generally harmful. This is exactly the kind of process Hume himself was much concerned to account for, with his principles of association.

The only other possibility is that the case of Rover and Jones is a case where passion outruns cognition—that is, Rover doesn't cognize Jones in any new way, beyond being an obstacle to the desired bone, but his frustration gains a physical inertia that carries him forward in attack mode, even once this cognition becomes baseless. This physical inertia is like a heart that continues pounding even after the shadow on the wall is proved to be that of a tree and not an intruder, or the sobbing that breaks out only after the missing child is found. Since Aquinas conceives of the passions as physio-psychological phenomena, he has every right to this possibility, as well—the blood boiling around Rover's heart takes a while to cool, even once its original cause has disappeared. It might seem the Humean has less right to this possibility, since she conceives of passionate motivation as a set of dispositions that tend to persist as long as, and only as long as, the belief that their object does not exist. I see no reason, however, why the Humean cannot include among these dispositions tendencies to inertial physical reactions—i.e., physical reactions that tend to persist for some time after said belief is abandoned.

Each of these stories relies only on differences in the passionate person's beliefs to specify "irascible" hope and explain how it can acquire a life of its own. I thus conclude that the Humean can accommodate the Thomistic distinction between concupiscible and irascible passions, by appealing to cognitions of or beliefs about instrumental relations and cognitions of the need for effort or good fortune if the object of desire is to be attained, or the object of aversion avoided.

This is Aquinas's analysis of hope:

> [I]n the object of hope, we may note four conditions. First, that it is something good; since properly speaking, hope regards only the good; in this respect, hope differs from fear, which regards evil. Secondly, that it is future; for hope does not regard that which is present and already possessed: in this respect, hope differs from joy, which regards a present good. Thirdly, *that it must be arduous and difficult to obtain, for we do not speak of anyone hoping for trifles, which are in one's power to have at any time: in this respect, hope differs from desire or cupidity, which regards the future good absolutely: wherefore it belongs to the concupiscible, while hope belongs to the irascible faculty.* Fourthly, that this difficult thing is something possible to obtain: for one does not hope for that which one cannot get at all: and, in this respect, hope differs from despair.[23]

The first condition tells us that hope involves desire (or attraction) and not aversion. The second condition contains a faulty inference: the fact that one does not hope for a present and possessed good does not entail that one hopes only for future goods. One can hope for past or present goods that one does not know the status of; later on, Aquinas is quite clear that the relevant statuses of the object have to do with what the hopeful person believes or knows to be the case, and not the actual temporal location of the object. That is, a person can hope for something that is objectively present (or past) but subjectively not known to be so (and she can also hope for something that is objectively bad, though subjectively perceived by her as good). The third condition is intended to identify hope as a distinctive, irascible motive force, but I have argued that there is no explanatory need to posit such a motivational power. We need only to specify certain doxastic or cognitive conditions. Finally, the fourth condition further specifies the doxastic condition on hope, establishing that we do not hope for outcomes we believe are impossible. We rather wish for them, or, as Aquinas says, despair of them. Aquinas's analysis thus appears to shrink to a version of the orthodox definition.

The Second Extreme: Calhoun and Seconding Practical Commitment

On the interpretation just reached, Aquinas's definition is a variant of the orthodox definition, and is therefore susceptible to the problems I presented in chapter 1. It also appears to undermine the possibility that hope has any

---

23   Ibid., 1a 2ae Q40 Art.1 (emphasis added).

special kind of sustaining power. Some authors see this apparent implication as a reason to reject the orthodox definition, but Cheshire Calhoun embraces it, arguing instead that we are often susceptible to an inflated view of hope's sustaining power. I will argue that she underestimates hope's sustaining power; for even under the orthodox definition, hope can not only "second" a preexisting commitment—as she says—but it can also strengthen existing commitments and give rise to new ones. Under the incorporation analysis, these influences acquire yet greater strength and stability.

Calhoun is most interested in what she calls "practical hopes," which are the hopes implicated in our long-term practical projects or commitments—namely, hopes for the success of these projects, including for the success of constitutive sub-plans and projects. These are her focus because she believes they are the hopes that matter most to us from the perspective of *agency*; they make use of our most sophisticated agential powers. Now, if the incorporation analysis is right, even hopes that are not "practical" in exactly Calhoun's sense involve sophisticated agential powers and can be of significance from the perspective of agency. Specifically, even the hope for a lucky outcome that one does not contemplate pursuing or integrating into a plan calls upon one's ability to treat considerations as practical reasons, and is a way of incorporating one's attraction to that outcome into one's imaginative, emotional, and planning life. I will set this point aside for now, however, and simply consider her argument's application to the definition of hope she defends.

"Hoping," Calhoun writes, "is an emotional attitude directed at a temporal unfolding of events that one prefers and believes possible."[24] Two points about this definition bear emphasizing. One is that Calhoun associates hope with a stronger endorsement of the hoped-for outcome than desire—hence the preferred "temporal unfolding of events." A hoped-for outcome is one that the hopeful person would prefer to see actualize, while it is possible to desire an outcome while preferring that it not actualize. Although this distinction between "preferring" in the temporal unfolding of events and "desiring" sounds something like the distinction between setting it as an end to bring about an outcome and simply being attracted to the outcome, there are some key differences. First, one can prefer that an outcome actualize without thereby setting out to bring it about—so Calhoun's definition is not the end-setting view I rejected at the end of chapter 2. Even more fundamentally, Calhoun does not clearly demarcate rational and subrational representations in the way that the latter distinction requires. So, for Calhoun, the relevant difference between hope and desire seems to amount something like the difference between seeing something as all-things-considered attractive and defeasibly attractive. Hope thus comes out as a narrower phenomenon than desire, but this is arguably still a variation of the orthodox definition.

24 Calhoun, "Hope Matters," ms 4.

The second point to emphasize about Calhoun's definition is that she takes seriously the dispositions of attention and imagination involved in desire (whether she considers desire a rational or subrational form of motivation). I argued in chapter 1 that, when Bovens insists that the orthodox definition should be supplemented with a mental imaging condition, he fails to take seriously the ways that desire or attraction engages the imagination. Calhoun's articulation of her version of the orthodox definition makes the imaginative engagement involved in hope quite clear. She writes:

> [H]ope is a pattern of *disattention* to evidence suggestive of the pursuit's possible or likely failure . . . hope involves the *imaginative projection of one's self into the future*; and hope typically is supported by a *hope narrative* that makes sense of one's disattending negative evidence and one's taking seriously the possibility of becoming the hoped-for future self.[25]

In this passage, she is specifically talking about practical hopes—hence the focus on evidence relevant to a *pursuit*, and the narrative regarding the *self* one hopes to become. Despite this focus, it is clear that she intends her arguments to stem from a *unified* theory of hope rather than a theory that treats practical hopes as different in kind from other hopes. I think, therefore, that she would extend these points to nonpractical hopes, as well, and maintain that, for example, the hope for good weather tomorrow involves dispositions to ignore evidence of bad weather, imagine good weather, and even construct a narrative to make it seem plausible that the weather will be good.

Calhoun argues that, in virtue of these constitutive elements, hope has a limited but significant sustaining power: hope "seconds" preexisting practical commitments. There are, she argues, three degrees of practical commitment: shot-taking, endeavoring, and totally investing in an end. The difference between these degrees is a matter of what it takes to induce one to reconsider the end. A person who totally invests in an end is unwilling to change course no matter what obstacles or setbacks she encounters; a person who endeavors to achieve an end will reconsider only as a result of fairly significant or frequent obstacles; and a person who only takes a shot will reconsider relatively easily.

According to Calhoun, the degree of a person's commitment determines how one's hope plays out. A person who only takes a shot at an end "imaginatively projects" herself into a future where she achieves it, but she does so only provisionally, prepared to stop if "evidence of likely failure starts coming in."[26] By contrast, those who endeavor are more committed, and will turn their imaginations away from their end only in the face of serious obstacles; while total investors are yet more stubborn. Hope seconds the preexisting

---

25   Ibid., p. 20.
26   Ibid., p. 22.

commitment through its effects on one's awareness of evidence relevant to the likely success or failure of one's project:

> Hope can second commitment, because hope, like other emotional atti-
> tudes, consists in part in a distinctive pattern of salience in our perceiv-
> ings, imaginings, and thinkings-about. . . . Hope, in short, focuses our
> imaginative eye on the desirability and possibility of succeeding in our
> pursuit, in spite of the disappointment of constitutive hopes along the
> way. Hoping thus seconds our commitment—whether it's a commitment
> to taking a shot, or to endeavoring, or to totally investing—by making
> salient the reasons for keeping to the commitment, and by disattending
> evidence that would incline us to think that we have reached the bar for
> what counts as too many or too large obstacles or uncertainties given the
> kind of commitment we've made. Hope thus delays reconsideration of our
> practical pursuits.[27]

So, while hope sustains us in our practical pursuits because it delays re-consideration of them, it delays them only insofar as the agent is already committed to her pursuit: it "seconds" her commitment. In relation to a trial, then, hope's sustaining power depends on whether and how much the sufferer is committed to striving to overcome or abide the trial. This is the extreme view at the opposite end of the spectrum from Aquinas's. Whereas Aquinas thinks hope is itself a kind of motive force, specially equipped to overcome obstacles, Calhoun argues that hope's sustaining power depends on an independent and preexisting commitment. I believe Calhoun overlooks some of the ways that hopeful imaginative activities can influence motivation and that hope can sustain a person, either in a practical pursuit or in the face of a trial she has no power to act against, without drawing exclusively on preexisting commitments. I do agree with her, however, that hope is not itself a *special kind* of motive force or power; hope is a matter of familiar forms of motivation: subrational attraction and rational end-setting. As I will now go on to argue, hope can also influence motivation through the hopeful person's *beliefs*, and thereby go beyond seconding preexisting practical commitments—but this does not make hope itself a special kind of motivational force.

Hopeful Fantasies and Sustenance

Hope, conceived under either the orthodox definition or the incorporation analysis, can influence both one's general sense of agency and one's particular exercises of agency. Both forms of influence stem primarily from the fact

---

27 Ibid., 26–27.

that hoping for an outcome means being disposed to fantasize about it, as I argued in the first chapter. What I have called "fantasies" are essentially the same as Calhoun's "imaginative projections," taking account also of the hope "narratives" she mentions—we agree that hoping for an outcome involves a disposition to imagine ways the outcome might actualize. Let's begin with the possible effects of such activities on one's general sense of agency.

In our fantasies, we may represent ourselves as more or less active. I will use the term "active fantasies" to refer to fantasies where one represents herself as active, and "passive fantasies" to refer to those where she represents herself as inactive. (I count a fantasy where one does not appear as a passive fantasy, unless it presupposes one's activity set the scene, as when I imagine a friend's pleasure upon finding the cobbler I secretly put in her fridge.) This self-representation may then seep past the boundaries of the fantasy and influence one's overall sense of agency. One's sense of agency may then have a range of effects on the ends one sets and how one pursues them. The princess whose hope to escape from her tower is expressed in extensive fantasies of rescue is far less likely to take steps toward freeing herself than the princess who fantasizes about escape routes. That is, I am postulating two linked causal mechanisms: fantasy affecting one's sense of agency and one's sense of agency affecting one's ability to overcome or abide a trial.

There is evidence for the latter mechanism. Coincidentally, this evidence comes from studies employing positive psychologist C. R. Snyder's "Hope Scale." Snyder and colleagues study a phenomenon they define as "a cognitive set that is based on a reciprocally-derived sense of agency (goal-directed determination) and pathways (planning to meet goals)."[28] This set is measured with a self-report instrument that taps the participant's beliefs about her abilities to set and achieve meaningful goals (e.g., "I meet the goals I set in life") and her abilities to figure out means to achieve those goals (e.g., "I can think of many ways to get the things in life that are most important to me").

Perhaps there are reasons to call this set of attitudes "hope" in a technical way, but it is clearly not the same attitude I have been discussing and refining by interrogating our intuitions about cases and counterexamples. The phenomenon Snyder studies is a set of attitudes *toward one's own agency*, while hope is an attitude taken toward many outcomes and not only toward one's agency. One could hope to be better at meeting her goals, or at figuring out ways to meet those goals, but being directed at such outcomes is certainly not a defining feature of hope. Additionally, there is a case to be made that one's sense of agency constitutes more than the beliefs reported by Snyder's Hope Scale. For example, beliefs about one's ability to effectively coordinate the pursuit of multiple ends, to prioritize ends consistent with one's values and

---

28   C. R. Snyder et al., "The Will and The Ways: Development and Validation of an Individual Differences Measure of Hope," *Journal of Personality and Social Psychology* 60 (1991): 57–85.

perhaps, even, to recognize when it would be better to abandon an end, seem plausible constituents of a sense of agency.

These qualifications aside, numerous studies validate Snyder's Hope Scale as tapping a reliable construct, and this instrument appears to give us access to at least the core elements of a sense of agency. Moreover, a number of studies using this instrument support my claim that a person's sense of agency affects her ability to overcome or abide a trial. For example, higher scores on the Hope Scale correlate to the selection of more numerous and more challenging goals, increased ability to overcome obstacles, and greater success in meeting goals.[29] A person with a stronger sense of agency is thus more likely to find a way through her trial.

The other part of my postulation about fantasy's influence on a person's ability to overcome or abide a trial is that fantasies can affect one's sense of agency. As far as I am aware, there is no direct and systematic empirical evidence for this postulate. There are a number of studies of mental simulation—which I will discuss later—that demonstrate a positive correlation between active fantasies and more effective planning, but they do not tell us whether this connection runs through the individual's sense of agency. This part of my claim thus remains speculative. However, it is not uncommon for people preparing for challenges to claim that imagining themselves surmounting an obstacle bolsters their confidence that they will succeed. Furthermore, active fantasies seem more likely to reveal new means to achieving desired goals than do passive fantasies. So it is plausible that active fantasizers find it easier to believe they are good at finding means than do passive fantasizers—because the results of their fantasies provide support for those beliefs. Hence, there are some conceptual and anecdotal reasons to think active fantasizing strengthens one's sense of agency and thereby one's ability to successfully contend with a trial.

Under either the orthodox definition or the incorporation analysis, hoping means being disposed to fantasize about the hoped-for outcome, and thereby susceptible to the forms of influence just discussed. Under the incorporation analysis, the hopeful person also stands ready to justify both her fantasies and an accompanying positive feeling of anticipation—so it seems likely these forms of influence will be both stronger and more stable. Moreover, the degree of activity of a hopeful person's fantasies is independent of the strength of her preexisting commitment to pursuing the hoped-for outcome. A serious endeavorer, for example, might use her fantasies primarily as a break from reality, imagining how great it would be if only she didn't have to work so hard to get what she wants. And a shot-taker might be an active fantasizer—perhaps because part of what she wants is to become a more dedicated and active agent. Even more, a person who is entirely passive

29 Ibid.

with regard to a hoped-for outcome might nevertheless entertain highly active fantasies about it. For example, someone who suffers from extreme self-doubt might be unable to muster the confidence to even take a shot at some highly desired but highly unlikely outcome, and yet be sufficiently self-aware that she regrets her self-sabotage. When she thinks about the hoped-for outcome, therefore, she tends to imagine herself as she wishes she were: actively pursuing it.

Trials of depression might often have this kind of structure. The depressed person strongly hopes for her depression to lift and knows there are certain active steps she needs to take to bring this about, even while her depression paralyzes her and makes the effort involved in taking those steps appear overwhelming. If she were at least able to *imagine* herself getting out of bed tomorrow, turning on the lights, and calling a friend, then this fantasy might be directly sustaining. It might sustain her by simply giving her a mental break from the onslaught of negative thoughts, and it could also—by the mechanisms I have sketched—causally bolster her sense of agency so that, one morning, she might find herself actually able throw back the covers.

Fantasies can also affect a hopeful person's agency in less global ways. As manifestations of attraction, fantasies are likely to focus on the features of the hoped-for outcome that make it attractive in the first place. For example, someone suffering from a debilitating illness and hoping for the return of health is likely to focus her fantasies on the very things that make health attractive, such as the absence of pain, ease of movement, the energy to pursue beloved pursuits, etc. However, fantasies are a kind of free-play of imagination, which can lead the fantasizer to notice or posit features she had not considered before. Because of their narrative structure, fantasies propose more or less complete accounts of how the world might be. They can thereby provide a hopeful person with new data that she may take as relevant to her situation. In particular, they can propose previously unconsidered attractive or aversive features of the hoped-for outcome.

Imagine, for example, a young writer having trouble conceiving a child. She is quite hopeful that she will become pregnant, and has various fantasies about becoming and being the mother of a small baby. One of these fantasies is a simple one: sitting on the front porch, working on her first novel, while the baby naps in a wind-up swing. As she pictures this scene, it occurs to her that becoming a mother could affect her writing in interesting ways, by giving her the experience of a new range of emotions. As it happens, this change strikes her as appealing, and motherhood becomes even more attractive to her than before.

It is worth being specific about the difference between how the attractive features of a hoped-for outcome appear in a fantasy, as opposed to how they appear "from within" the attraction. As I argued in chapter 2, attraction is not only a disposition to fantasy; it also disposes one to certain patterns of attention and perception (and Calhoun agrees, as we saw above, although she does not explicitly distinguish attraction and rational desire). So, when I am attracted to having another cup of coffee, my mind drifts to thoughts of coffee and if, say, the coffee is before me, its attractive features become more salient—I notice its appealing smell, the comforting curl of steam, etc. The way these features appear to me is importantly different from the way attractive features appear in a fantasy. From inside an attraction, the attractive features of an outcome appear as facts about the world; there is no distance between one's view of the world and this appearance. The worlds proposed by fantasies, by contrast, appear to some degree distant from the actual world, and it takes a judgment on the part of the fantasizer to bring them together. The writer must believe her fantasy has, at least in the relevant respects, accurately represented a way the world could be. Only then does the possibility of the change in her writing become something that can enhance her attraction to motherhood.

If she makes this judgment, her hope could play an important and unique sustaining role in the writer's trial. She sees this fantasizing as a legitimate rational activity, and it makes motherhood out to be even more appealing than she had originally thought. Her hope thereby reinforces itself and gives her a potential new reason to commit to her struggle—if she considers this new attraction a reason to adopt the end of pursuing motherhood.

Again, then, we see hope going beyond merely seconding a preexisting commitment to an end. Since hope, manifested in a fantasy, can generate new attractions to the hoped-for outcome, it can also generate *new reasons* to commit to pursuing that outcome. At least, this is true if it is also true that attractions sometimes provide practical reasons, as I discussed in chapter 2. Through this process, hope could even generate a decisive reason to commit to this project. Thus a person suffering a trial could start out seeing the end of the trial as attractive but too far-fetched to merit much of an effort; and then, through her fantasies, wind up attaching even greater value to overcoming the trial, to the point where she decides that it is worth the effort after all. For example, the writer's hopeful fantasy might be what it takes to convince her to pursue adoption or infertility treatment.

The new attraction and new reason I have imagined being generated by the writer's hopeful fantasy are, admittedly, *motivated*—their motivational power derives from that of preexisting attractions and ends (namely, an attraction and commitment to improving her writing). So we might wonder whether a hopeful fantasy can generate an *unmotivated* attraction and thereby a *noninstrumental* reason to pursue the hoped-for outcome. It seems to me it can. Consider another story about the writer where she imagines an intrinsic feature of motherhood—the deep emotional attachment that some mothers feel to their children, which is arguably *partly constitutive* of motherhood for these women.[30] Thus, a fantasy proposing that emotional attachment is a constitutive part of motherhood could generate an unmotivated attraction; and this attraction could even be a decisive consideration that a woman takes as sufficient reason to finally adopt the end of becoming a mother.

An interesting complication now arises, however. Even though fantasies have an egoistic function and are therefore likely to focus on the attractive features of hoped-for outcomes, they are also narrative forms of imaginative free-play, and there is nothing in principle preventing aversive features from making their appearance. Depending on the sort of person the writer is, and how she thinks about her writing, the possibility that becoming a mother will change her writing might appear a *negative* feature, as could the possibility of deep emotional attachment to a helpless creature. The fantasy could therefore cause her to form an aversion to something she previously found purely attractive—this aversion could even be, for her, a decisive reason to abandon or never adopt the end of becoming a mother.

Or consider another example: Once, at the height of the (latest) housing bubble, I bid on a fixer-upper home. Knowing I was unlikely to win the bid, I still very much hoped to, and often fantasized about the changes and improvements I would make to the house. These fantasies led me to realize what a great deal of work would follow, if I won the bid. I believe it was in part this realization—which perhaps I understood in the abstract before, but which was made visceral by imagining myself cleaning, sanding, painting, and so on—that allowed me to be only slightly disappointed when I was outbid. My fantasies weakened my attraction; I came to represent winning the bid as less attractive than before. My situation wasn't really a trial for me, but it is easy enough to impose the same structure on a story of a trial: for example, an unemployed person might first focus all her hope on getting rehired by her former employer but then, in imagining returning to her workplace, recall how miserable the job made her.

In addition to strengthening or weakening the hopeful person's sense of agency, and strengthening or weakening one's attraction to the hoped-for outcome, hopeful fantasies can influence one's beliefs about possible means to realizing one's hope. On the one hand, fantasies can help us discover means to bringing about hoped-for ends. Imagine a high school student who hopes desperately to go to a certain college, because she believes it is the only way to get out of her dead-end town and make something of herself.

---

30 Note that I say the feeling is constitutive of motherhood *for these women*—it is, for them, part of what it means to be the mothers that they are. I am not claiming that this feeling is constitutive of motherhood *per se*.

Unfortunately, she hasn't always been so determined, and her grades and accomplishments have been, until recently, mediocre. She is at a loss as to how she could possibly realize her hope until, one day, daydreaming about the application process, she imagines an alumnus interviewer questioning her previous performance and defensively constructs a narrative explaining her development as a person and a student. She realizes this is the story she should tell in her personal essay. On the other hand, as a result of fantasizing about her strategy for achieving a hoped-for outcome, a person could come to believe it will be ineffective, or too difficult, or in conflict with her values. Our student might realize she doesn't have a good explanation for her past performance—she was just lazy.

Contingent Sustenance

I have been arguing that hopeful fantasies are able to sustain us through our trials by strengthening our sense of agency, by proposing new reasons to stick to a struggle, and by proposing new means to success in one's struggle. These forms of sustenance do not depend on one's previous commitments—they can strengthen a weak commitment, and even give rise to a commitment where there was none before. This is true if one adopts the orthodox definition of hope, and even more so under the terms of the incorporation analysis, for the reasons discussed in the previous sections. Thus, I think Calhoun's claim that hope only seconds preexisting commitment underestimates the motivational power of hope, just as Aquinas's treatment of hope as a special irascible force overestimates it.

Calhoun is much closer to the truth than Aquinas is, however, because Aquinas is mistaken about the nature of hope's sustaining power. It is not a distinctive kind of motivational force, or an exercise of a special power that is better equipped to deal with obstacles than ordinary desire, or than subrational attraction and rational desire. Instead, it involves these standard forms of motivation, expressed in imagination in such a way that one may find sustenance in them. Moreover, the motivational influences I have identified in this chapter are all essentially *doxastic*: they are a matter of discovering or coming to believe certain propositions to be true—that the hoped-for outcome has yet further attractive features, that previously unconsidered means might work, that one is a more capable agent than one had previously thought. Thus, insofar as Calhoun's main concern was to establish that hope is not the font of a special causal power, her position and mine are the same in spirit, if not identical in the letter.

Now, an important qualification has come out in the course of my arguments: hopeful fantasies are only *contingently* sustaining. They can also propose reasons to *give up* a struggle, *doubt* the effectiveness of one's means or plans, and *lose confidence* in one's effectiveness as an agent. These contingencies are borne out by a number of psychological studies. Let us take a quick look at this literature.

There is a decent amount of psychological literature addressing the influences fantasizing can have on particular exercises of agency. Note first that recent work in neuropsychology suggests "daydreaming" or "mindwandering" is our baseline psychological state, against which focus on the present moment arises as an exception.[31] These categories, "daydreaming" and "mindwandering," are broad, and include in addition to the narrative egoistic activity I have called "fantasizing," activities like recalling past experiences and list-making. Nevertheless, many of the studies establishing connections between different forms of daydreaming and motivation are based on surveys that instruct participants to imagine desirable events unfolding, and the resulting literature speaks directly to the arguments I have made about hopeful fantasies.

Generally speaking, it is well established that mentally simulating desirable or planned events unfolding motivates one to promote those events, and increases one's chance of success. We see such results, for example, in studies of athletes' use of "mental practice" whereby they imagine successfully performing the physical movements needed to win an upcoming competition.[32] Recent studies refine the general connection between mental simulation and motivation in three interesting ways.

First, in two studies of students preparing for exams, Taylor et al. found that mentally simulating the process of studying led to both improved study habits and higher grades, while mentally simulating the mere outcome (the achievement of a high grade) did not. Indeed, one of the two studies found a correlation between outcome-simulation and lower grades, compared to the grades of a control group that was not instructed to engage in any mental simulation at all. They also found that the likely explanation for these results was that the process simulation both reduced anxiety and *facilitated planning*. As I speculated above, it appears some fantasies are better than others for discovering means and working through strategies.[33]

A second refinement comes from Oettingen et al., who ran a series of studies that identified important differences between the motivational effects of mentally simulating a desirable event series while simultaneously taking note of the obstacles reality poses to that series, versus simply simulating the

31   Adrienne Lapidos, "Daydream Control and Psychological Health" (Garden City, NY: Adelphi University, The Institute of Advanced Psychological Studies, 2008).

32   L. Curry and C. R. Snyder, "Hope Takes the Field: Mind Matters in Athletic Performances," in *Handbook of Hope: Theory, Measures, and Applications*, C. R. Snyder, ed. (Academic Press, 2000), 243–60.

33   Shelley E. Taylor, et. al. "Harnessing the Imagination," *American Psychologist* 53.4 (April 1998): 429–39.

events. In the former case, participants were motivated to initiate the events to a degree responsive to their assessment of the events' probability. If they believed they likely could initiate the events, they were highly motivated; if they believed their success was unlikely, they were less motivated. By contrast, participants who simulated the desirable events without the simultaneous reality check were motivated to a moderate degree, regardless their assessment of the odds. It seems, then, that when we consciously attend to the relation between the world a fantasy proposes and the real world, the fantasy better facilitates effective deliberation and implementation of our choices.[34]

Finally, Thomas Langens found that the motivational effects of fantasies are mediated by whether or not the fantasizer is "high in achievement motivation." Achievement motivation is a form of motivation that is driven by the need for excellence, and Langens used a standard measurement protocol that codes participants' descriptions of picture cues, looking for concern for standards of excellence. Langens found that, among first-year university students high in achievement motivation, the stronger their commitments to staying in contact with friends and succeeding in their studies, the more fantasies about these goals promoted their pursuit and attainment of these goals. This was not true of participants not highly motivated by concerns for excellence and achievement. That is, "positive daydreaming mediated between goal commitment and goal attainment for individuals high, but not for those low in achievement motivation."[35] Langens points out that other studies have shown that individuals high in achievement motivation have a "realistic, down-to-earth outlook on life." Here, then, we have some evidence that certain character traits, such as achievement motivation and the tendency to evaluate the realism of one's fantasies, may affect how fantasies influence one's particular exercises of agency.

These various results fit well with my suggestion that one of the important things fantasies do is propose worlds. A more realistic fantasizer is more likely to discover genuinely attractive features of a hoped-for outcome and thereby genuine reasons to pursue that outcome, as well as more plausible means to this end. Her fantasies, in other words, are more likely to be relevant to her exercise of effective agency in pursuit of the hoped-for outcome. Similarly, a person who consciously assesses the reality of her fantasies is likely to find her fantasies useful resources for deliberation; while a

34 G. Oettingen and D. Mayer, "The Motivating Function of Thinking about the Future: Expectations versus Fantasies. *Journal of Personality and Social Psychology* 83.5 (November 2002): 1198–212. G. Oettingen, H. Pak, and K. Schnetter, "The Self-Regulation of Goal Setting: Turning Free Fantasies about the Future into Binding Goals," *Journal of Personality and Social Psychology* 80.5 (May 2001): 736–53.

35 Thomas Langens, "Daydreaming Mediates between Goal Commitments and Goal Attainment in Individuals High in Achievement Motivation," *Imagination, Cognition, and Personality* 22.2 (2003): 103–15.

person who instead indulges in flights of fancy for the sake of entertainment or escape, and without concern for their reality, is less likely to find useful material.

So, both conceptual arguments and empirical data strongly support the conclusion that, while hopeful fantasies can provide crucial forms of sustenance to people dealing with trials, there is no guarantee that they will do so. Returning, then, to the popular idea that hope has a special sustaining power, we see that there is an important sense in which this notion is valid, but that the estimate of this power is apt to be inflated. For, right alongside this view travels the companion notion that hope is *always a good thing*. There are many reasons one might think hope is essentially good, but no doubt much of the praise people heap on the attitude is due to the notion that it always bolsters agency—both globally and specifically. We should, however, be very skeptical of this notion, and equally skeptical of the unquestioningly positive assessment of hope it grounds.

An Example: "Self-Help" and Self-Sabotage

As Barbara Ehrenreich documents in her book, *Bright-Sided,* "visualization" is one of the core strategies recommended by the "positive thinking" movement in America.[36] Career coaches, self-help authors, cancer support groups, business motivation consultants, adherents of the "prosperity gospel": all recommend imagining what you want or need as an important strategy for getting it. The striking thing about this recommendation, in light of the above examination of fantasy and its potential effects on agency, is that one is almost always instructed to imagine *having* the desired outcome, or to simply picture the desired object; positive thinkers almost never recommend imagining *how to get* the desired object or how to bring about the desired outcome.

For example, Wallace D. Wattles, a member of the "New Thought" movement during the early part of the twentieth century, whose writing remains popular in present-day self-help movements, writes:

> See the things you want as if they were actually around you all the time. See yourself as owning and using them. Make use of them in imagination, just as you will use them when they are your tangible possessions. Dwell upon your mental picture until it is clear and distinct, and then take the mental attitude of ownership toward everything in that picture. Take possession

---

36   Barbara Ehrenreich, *Bright Sided: How Positive Thinking Is Undermining America* (New York: Henry Holt, 2009).

of it, in mind, in the full faith that it is actually yours. Hold to this mental ownership. Do not waiver for an instant in the faith that it is real.[37]

At the same time, you are to avoid all negative thoughts, especially thoughts or images of poverty, need, and want. You are not to watch the news, or listen to stories of people in need. The "law of attraction" will bring to you whatever you think about. The book is, frankly, a recipe for producing disengaged, disaffected, self-absorbed citizens (and it is all underwritten by the claim that you have a "right" to be rich, and that what God wants of you is that you become rich). Given what we have seen about the ways that fantasies can affect agency, it is also a recipe for *frustration*. Fantasies focused on outcome achievement rather than process are unmotivating, possibly demotivating; fantasies that do not include oneself contributing to the way events unfold may undermine agency across the board; fantasies that go unchecked against reality (like the reality that you are not, in fact, a multi-millionaire church leader) produce a degree of motivation unresponsive to the odds.

The visualizations one often finds recommended for people with cancer are not entirely process-free, but the processes one is to imagine are not ones that will engage one's agency or help one find a way to live well with cancer. (I hurry to add that "living well" with cancer does not necessarily mean living happily or peacefully.) The website, "Healing Cancer Naturally," recommends, for example, that the patient imagine the following:[38]

> A white light entering the body, bringing in energy, coursing through the body, then leaving the body and taking with it the 'bad stuff'—pain, tension, discomfort, or cancer cells. Or . . . white blood cells as 'knights on white horses' riding through the body attacking and destroying cancer cells. (Altman and Sarg, 2000, 141)

> Cancer as small, easily squashed creatures being lanced by white [blood cells] knights on horses. [Imagine the] goodness and purity of the immune system. (Jeanne Achterberg)

> Cancer cells as misfits who do not belong, always fighting for more power because they are aberrations and they don't know love and they are lonely.

---

37 Wallace Wattles, *The Wisdom Of Wallace D. Wattles: Including "The Science Of Getting Rich," "The Science Of Being Great," and "The Science Of Being Well"* (SoHo Books: 2011), 22. To be fair, Wattles does not explicitly recommend passivity. A great deal of his book touts the importance of acting. The thought he recommends, however, is of the outcome achievement rather than process variety. Moreover, his action recommendations are disturbingly vague and seem to add up to doing your present job well.

38 "Healing Cancer Naturally," last accessed January 30th, 2012: http://www.healingcancernaturally.com/.

So any decision I make about treatment I must temper with love, love for them no matter what they try to do to me. I envision little angels stroking them, blowing on them sweet baby's breath to cool their fire. (Linda Lewandowski)

Now, these kinds of visualizations can of course have a relaxing effect on one's mind and body—they can make one feel better; and that can be useful in dealing with the enormous social, physical, and mental stresses of cancer. But these are *not* the kind of fantasies that might help one find a new approach to treatment, or find activities that might make one's illness more bearable.[39]

By encouraging visualizations of angels and knights on horseback, we risk training people to hope in ways that promise, ultimately, to make them more passive, less effective agents. Our imagination is a powerful resource, but not because it can magically attract what we want or heal our bodies. Rather, the power of imagination lies in its ability to explore the world and its possibilities in a creative, sometimes surprising way. We could do better in harnessing this resource. This is not to say that passive fantasy is never a good or useful thing—but insofar as we think hope should inspire people to take stock of reality and take action, we should question movements that teach people to engage in hopeful imaginings that are likely to increase passivity.

Summary

Insofar as it relies on the belief that hope has a special power to sustain us through our greatest trials, the popular conviction that hope is a virtue gets something right, but this notion should not be taken too far. The paradigmatic hopeful activities of fantasizing about a hoped-for outcome and feeling positive anticipation of its fulfillment can influence the hopeful person's deliberation and motivational commitments through a variety of vectors. This influence goes beyond that of preexisting ends or practical commitments, and certainly has the potential to stengthen a person's ability to abide or even overcome extreme challenges to her welfare and flourishing. However, this influence is not itself a unique kind of motivational force, such as Aquinas's "irascible" passions are; it is simply the way that hopeful activities—which are expressions of standard motivational representations (attraction and end-setting)—can affect one's sense of agency and perception of reasons in the world. Moreover, these hopeful activities also have the potential to

---

39 They are also all loaded in some disturbing ways, particularly for women, who are the primary targets of the idea that one should find a way to feel positive about one's cancer. Apparently, when faced with the scary Big-C, one should fall back on being rescued by knights? Or, even, learn to *love* the cancer cells?

de-motivate and, thereby, it is reasonable to infer, make it more difficult to cope with a trial.

In the next chapter, I turn from the sustaining power of hope, as it is generally construed, to the potential of a specific kind of hope. Drawing on Immanuel Kant's and Gabriel Marcel's important accounts of religious hope, I argue that this hope has a number of characteristics that give it a noncontingent sustaining power, a power that goes beyond what we have seen in the present chapter—and thereby merits the label "faith." After identifying these characteristics, I consider the possibility that some secular hopes may share them. I consider, that is, the possibility of secular faith.

Faith and Sustenance without Contingency

What is the relation between hope and faith? According to Aquinas, they both ultimately take communion with God as their object. They are nevertheless distinct, because they target different aspects of that communion:

> [H]ope and faith make man adhere to God as to a principle wherefrom certain things accrue to us. Now we derive from God both knowledge of truth and the attainment of perfect goodness. Accordingly faith makes us adhere to God, as the source whence we derive the knowledge of truth, since we believe that what God tells us is true: while hope makes us adhere to God, as the source whence we derive perfect goodness, i.e., in so far as, by hope, we trust to the Divine assistance for obtaining happiness.[1]

Hope targets an outcome conceived as good, and thereby relies on God as the efficient cause of all goodness, while faith is a trust in God's word as truth.

This way of thinking about the contrast between hope and faith is clearly very different from contemporary popular usage of the terms "hope" and "faith." As discussed in the first chapter, we generally think of faith and hope as potentially secular attitudes that differ from one another in that faith is a more *confident* attitude than hope; hope is consistent with precautionary measures against its own disappointment, while faith is not. In this chapter, I set out to analyze faith as a variant of hope, and to determine both the rational restrictions on faith and the distinctive value of faith, particularly in relation to the ways it might support people in times of trial.

Chief Plenty Coups and Unimaginable Hope

In his book, *Radical Hope, Ethics in the Face of Cultural Devastation,* Jonathan Lear argues that Plenty Coups, the last great Chief of the Crow nation, possessed and put into practice a uniquely virtuous form of hope when he led

---

1 Aquinas, *Summa Theologiae,* 2a 2ae Q17 A7

the Crow people to relinquish their hunter-warrior life, align with Europeans in a war against the Sioux and Cheyenne tribes, voluntarily move onto reservations, and seek new ways to flourish as Crow people. His argument is that Plenty Coups' hope was both an expression and a transformation of courage, but that will not be my focus here. Instead, I aim to show that the hope Lear identifies has a kind of essential sustaining power lacked by hope in general, and that it has this power because it targets an outcome that is, for the hopeful person, *unimaginable*. I then draw from Immanuel Kant's and Gabriel Marcel's discussions of religious hope, in order to develop a detailed account of unimaginable hope, and to argue that it is best conceived as a kind of *faith*. Of course, both Kant and Marcel have in mind a specifically religious form of hope, and, in fact, Plenty Coups' hope was also religious—it was grounded in a spiritual vision he had as a young man, and it relied on the Crow people's shared belief that they were the favored people of the god *Ah-badt-dadt-deah*. However, Lear also suggests such a hope could be secularized—i.e., there is a form of faith available to atheists as well, and it is one that constitutes a virtuous and sustaining response to cultural collapse. I follow up on this suggestion, to arrive at a hope that targets a *contingently unimaginable outcome*. This, I argue, is what secular faith must be, if it is to be anything.[2]

Let's begin with Plenty Coups' situation. Before the arrival of the white man, the Crow led a nomadic life structured around hunting buffalo and warring with enemies. To flourish as a Crow was to lead a life defined by these practices; everything—children's play and education, meal preparation, the Sun Dance, the Tobacco ritual, tending horses, the planting and counting of coup sticks—was defined in relation to this *telos*: the hunter-warrior life. When the white men arrived, the buffalo began to disappear, and with them the possibility of a life as a hunter of buffalo. The white men also undermined the Crow way of being a warrior, as they shunted tribes onto reservations and imposed European conceptions of property on the "New World"—for example, declaring the act of capturing an enemy tribe's horses "theft," when it previously would have been a valorous accomplishment, a "counting of coups." They slaughtered horses and stole the Crow's children. The Crow nation faced the complete collapse of their defining way of life and thus the inability to *conceptualize* or *imagine* a way of going forward that would qualify as flourishing or even surviving for the Crow people *as Crow*, with their particular form of life. Any hope for the Crow to survive *as Crow* was, in a certain sense, unimaginable.

Here is, in brief, the story of Plenty Coups' hope. When Plenty Coups was nine years old, and the implications of the white men's arrival were still

---

2 Here, then, I strongly disagree with Mittleman, who argues that secular hope, if it does not illicitly smuggle in religious convictions, is ultimately shallow and unstable. *Hope in a Democratic Age*, especially chapter 5.

somewhat at the fringes of Crow consciousness, he went out into nature and sought a vision. This was common practice. He took a sweat-bath, fasted, and chopped off a piece of his finger in order to appear pitiable to *Ah-badt-dadt-deah*. During his second night, he had a complex dream in which he saw the buffalo disappear and a tremendous storm blow over all of the trees in the forest, "but one." A voice then told him that the remaining tree was the home of the Chickadee, whose virtue is to listen and learn from the successes and failure of others. The voice told him to develop his mind and be like the Chickadee. Upon Plenty Coups' return, the tribe interpreted the dream as a message that the white man would, in Plenty Coups' lifetime, "take and hold this country": "The tribes who have fought the white man have all been beaten, wiped out. By listening as the Chickadee listens we may escape this and keep our lands."[3]

This was the hope that led Plenty Coups and his people forward: that by being like the Chickadee, they could adapt to the oncoming storm and find a way to live after the buffalo left and their lives became unrecognizable. As Lear interprets it, Plenty Coups' hope was inconceivable or *unimaginable*. It was not that he could not imagine a life, generally speaking, of farming rather than hunting—it was that he could not imagine such a life as a *Crow* way of life, because the Crow were, by definition, hunters. To hope simply that the Crow might survive by becoming farmers would be, in part, to hope that the Crow might survive by ceasing to be Crow. Instead (at least as Lear interprets him), he hoped the Crow could find a new way of being Crow—and this was to hope for an outcome that outstripped his available concepts of the Crow.

Lear calls Plenty Coups' hope "radical." I believe he means this term to capture both the unimaginable aspect I have just described, and also this hope's connection with courage. For my purposes here, I want to focus on the unimaginable aspect and its implications, and so will stick with the label, "unimaginable hope" to indicate a hope for an outcome that outstrips the hopeful person's concepts in such a way that he cannot imagine or conceive of it.

Unimaginable hope is, I am going to argue in this chapter, different from the hopes discussed in the previous chapter, because it is noncontingently sustaining in two ways. First, a person who forms an unimaginable hope and understands that it is unimaginable will not be vulnerable to the demotivating factors discussed in chapter 3—she will not attempt to fantasize or imagine experiencing an outcome that she understands is beyond her conceptual resources. Of course, this also means she will not have available the contingent motivating and sustaining benefits of hopeful fantasy; instead, her hope will sustain her in virtue of its constituent desire or attraction to the outcome, and through the feelings and plans she sees as justified. This is why it is important that unimaginable hope is noncontingently sustaining in a second

3   Lear, *Radical Hope*, (Cambridge, MA: Harvard University Press, 2006), 66–75.

way: it is immune to empirical disappointment. Nothing in the hopeful person's experience need count as a reason to stop desiring the unimaginable outcome, or to stop seeing its chances as licensing a feeling of anticipation and hedged reliance on the outcome in her plans, or to stop treating her desire as sufficient justification for this feeling and planning. That is to say, nothing in the hopeful person's experience need count as evidence that her hope is fruitless.

Kant on the Highest Good and Morally Obligatory Hope

With this sketch of unimaginable hope, I now turn to Kant, from whom I draw the idea that genuinely unimaginable hope has a special kind of theoretical or epistemic rational license, such that the hopeful person has rational permission to adopt a certain meta-confidence toward her hopefulness. This meta-confidence turns hope into a form of faith.[4]

Famously, Kant presents his overall critical project as answering three questions: "All the interests of reason (the speculative as well as the practical) are united in the following three questions: 1. What can I know? 2. What ought I to do? 3. What may I hope?"[5] Over the course of several books, he answers these questions: 1. We can know only the sensible world cognized through the categories—our most fundamental, *a priori* concepts—though we must admit the possibility of a world beyond our ken. 2. We ought to conform our actions to the moral law, the Categorical Imperative as it is expressed in the Formulas of Universal Law, Humanity, and the Kingdom of Ends. 3. We may hope for immortality and the existence of God. Kant's claim is that hopes for immortality and the existence of God have a special kind of rational sanction.

That Kant's third critical question should be as fundamental as the other two is not obvious. Rational knowledge and action clearly are the defining aims of theoretical and practical reason, respectively, but how does *hope* fit into the picture? We can see why Kant included the third question by considering what he means by an "interest" of reason. An interest of reason is something that *determines* reason's activity; that is, it is an end for the sake of which we use our rational faculties. A purely rational interest is an end dictated by the very nature of these faculties. Theoretical reason, by its nature, seeks knowledge. Practical reason, by its nature, produces rational action. Conformity with the moral law describes pure practical reason's interest in

---

4 For a thorough examination of Kant's full account of hope, and an examination of its implications, see Sidney Axinn, *The Logic of Hope: Extensions of Kant's View of Religion* (Amsterdam: Rodopi, 1994).

5 Immanuel Kant, *Critique of Practical Reason*, Paul Guyer and Alan Wood, trans. (Cambridge: Cambridge University Press, 1998), B 832–B 833.

general terms, but the Categorical Imperative also gives us two specific rationally necessary ends: our own virtue, and others' happiness. These two ends in turn give us the idea of a "final and complete" end of practical reason, which is the "Highest Good," or the end that would result from the perfect pursuit of our two rationally necessary ends.[6]

Two features of these specific ends dictated by the Categorical Imperative are essential to the idea of the Highest Good. First, by "happiness," Kant means not a state of pleasure or contentment, but the achievement of our ends. So our duty is not to help people feel good, but to support them in the completion of their projects (though we are not to excessively compromise our own projects in the process). Second, virtue restricts happiness; we are not to sacrifice virtue for the sake of either pursuing our own optional ends or promoting others' happiness. Thus, we should promote only others' *permissible* ends. The Highest Good, then, is a world where everyone always conforms to the Categorical Imperative, and the result is that, first, everyone is perfectly virtuous and so, second, everyone achieves all of her ends (since the virtuous person's ends are all permissible). Kant sometimes characterizes the second part of the Highest Good in terms of happiness proportional to virtue, or each person attaining happiness to the degree she is worthy of it. However, since everyone in the world of the Highest Good is perfectly virtuous, everyone has only permissible ends, and so they in fact attain all of their ends—they are perfectly happy, because perfectly virtuous in a world of perfectly virtuous people.[7]

The Highest Good is an *interest* of practical reason—insofar as we are rational, we have it as an end. This is part of Kant's answer to the second critical question, "What ought I to do?"—I ought to make the Highest Good my end. The ideal nature of the Highest Good leads him to his third critical question and its answer. Kant presents what is known as "the moral argument" for religious hope in somewhat different forms, in multiple places.[8] For my purposes, the differences are not important, and I will focus on his discussion in *The Critique of Practical Reason*. Here, he argues that the possibility of the Highest Good presupposes both one's own immortality—one needs infinite

---

6   Ibid., 5: 120.

7   That is to say, sometimes Kant focuses on the obligation to pursue a *just* world, where virtue is apportioned to happiness and, sometimes he focuses on the obligation to pursue an *ideal* world, where everyone is perfectly happy and perfectly virtuous. I think that, in the latter, perfect happiness still *follows from* perfect virtue, and the difference between these two conceptions of the Highest Good is not important to the points I want to make here, which concern the rationally legitimate attitude to take toward the presuppositions of the Highest Good.

8   In addition to the discussion in the *Critique of Practical Reason*, the moral argument for God appears in Immanuel Kant, *Critique of Pure Reason*, Allen Wood and Paul Guyer, eds. (Cambridge: Cambridge University Press, 1999), A795=B823ff; and *Religion within the Limits of Reason Alone* in *Religion and Rational Theology*, Allen Wood and George di Giovanni, eds. and trans. (Cambridge: Cambridge University Press, 1996), 6: 66, 60–75, 70.

time to achieve perfect virtue, because we all start out radically evil—and also a "Providence which knows each one's desert and ultimately apportions happiness according to it."[9] As Allen Wood argues, this argument has the potential to put the rational agent in something of a fix. If the Highest Good is a morally necessary end, and if it presupposes human immortality and the existence of God, then we are in some sense *morally committed* to the propositions that we have immortal souls and that God exists. That is to say, we would be in some kind of practically incoherent state if we refused to accept, in some sense, these propositions. Yet Kant also thinks these propositions lack "sufficient objective grounds"—that is, either a priori or a posteriori evidence that they are likely to be true.[10] Practical and theoretical reason thus appear in conflict.

The resolution is, of course, that this "commitment" or "acceptance," which Kant most often refers to as *Glaube*, cannot be the equivalent of contemporary philosophical conceptions of belief; it has to be an attitude that can be legitimate in the absence of evidence proving the truth of its object proposition. I now want to suggest that this attitude strongly resembles hope as I have analyzed it as a mode of incorporation.

Kant calls the propositions that we have immortal souls and that God exists "postulates of practical reason," and they are his answer to his third critical question, "What may I hope?"[11] Kant says a postulate of practical reason is "a *theoretical* proposition, though not one demonstrable as such, insofar as

---

9 Kant, *Critique of Practical Reason*, 5: 121–32. There is a substantial literature dedicated to interpreting and this and the argument in *Religion within the Limits of Reason Alone*, which I will not attempt to go into here. Some important major discussions include: Allen Wood, *Kant's Moral Religion* (Ithaca, NY and London: Cornell University Press, 1970); Wood, *Kant's Rational Theology* (Ithaca, NY and London: Cornell University Press, 1978); and Wood, "Rational Theology, Moral Faith and Religion," *The Cambridge Companion to Kant*, Paul Guyer, ed. (Cambridge: Cambridge University Press, 1992) 394–416; Onora O'Neill, *Kant on Reason and Religion* (The Tanner Lectures on Human Values, 1997), Grethe B. Patterson, ed. (Salt Lake City, UT: University of Utah Press, 1997), 269–308; Otfried Höffe, "What May I Hope?—The Philosophy of History and Religion,"in *Immanuel Kant*, Marshall Farrier, trans. (Albany, NY: State University of New York Press, 1994), 193–209; Paul Guyer, "From a Practical Point of View: Kant's Conception of a Postulate of Pure Practical Reason," *Kant on Freedom, Law and Happiness* (Cambridge, Cambridge University Press, 2000), 333–71; Frederick Beiser, "Moral Faith and the Highest Good," *The Cambridge Companion to Kant and Modern Philosophy*, Paul Guyer, ed. (Cambridge: Cambridge University Press, 2006), 588–629.

10 See Andrew Chignell, "Belief in Kant," *Philosophical Review* 116.3 (2007): 323–60; and "Kant's Concepts of Justification," *Noûs* 41.1 (2007): 33–63.

11 In *Religion within the Limits of Reason Alone*, Kant suggests that the answer to his question "What may I hope?" is not the practical postulates, but the doctrines of social and historical progress, and individual grace. (See also Mittleman, *Hope in a Democratic Age*, 167–81.) However, his earlier work strongly intimates that the practical postulates are his answer, and it is common in Kant scholarship to treat them as such. See for example, Onora O'Neill, *Kant on Reason and Religion*, 269–308. There is a third postulate: that our wills are autonomous. However, this postulate derives not from an obligation to pursue the Highest Good, but from the conditions for the possibility

it is attached inseparably to an a priori unconditionally valid *practical* law."[12] The key, then, is that we are *theoretically licensed*, and *practically justified* in committing to the postulates.

We have seen the practical justification: the obligation to pursue the Highest Good, and its presupposition of the postulates. Now consider the theoretical license. The concepts involved in the practical postulates are of outcomes "unimaginable" in much the same way as Plenty Coups' concept of Crow flourishing. Nothing in our possible experience could satisfy these concepts, because they outstrip the basic categories shaping that experience. Thus, experience can never prove or disprove the existence of an immortal soul or God.[13] Nor, Kant argues in the first *Critique*, are there any sound *a priori* arguments that prove or disprove their existence.[14] As far as theoretical reason is concerned, then, the most rational attitude toward them is a principled agnosticism. The commitment we are morally obliged to take toward the practical postulates thus has a special theoretical *license* or *permission*: theoretical reason has nothing to say against (or for) this commitment, as long as it does not purport to be a theoretically grounded commitment.

This commitment is supposed to be an entirely practical attitude. Indeed, Kant characterizes it as *willing*:

> The upright man may well say, I *will* that there be a God . . . [and] that my duration be endless; I stand by this, without paying attention to rationalizations, however little I may be able to answer them or to oppose them with others more plausible, and I will not let this belief [*Glaube*] be taken from me[.][15]

Now, willing is setting an end, so Kant can't quite mean this literally—we cannot set the end of bringing God or our own immortal souls into existence. That is to say, we don't literally will the conditions of our willing. However, if we treat this language as somewhat figurative, it is suggestive of a justifying relation. Kant has argued that we need to rely on the practical postulates in our pursuit of the Highest Good, so it seems to me his description of the "upright man" is of someone who treats the theoretical status of the postulates as

---

of moral obligation in general. Presumably, this difference is why Kant identifies only immortality and God as objects of hope. Our commitment to the possibility of autonomy is stronger than hope.

12 Kant, *Critique of Practical Reason*, 5:122.

13 Thus Axinn argues that, for Kant, it is reasonable to place hope in a transcendental object only so long as one does not "use" rather than "mention" the hope—that is, one is free to orient one's mind and motives toward the transcendental object and "mention" it to oneself (and others), but one may not "use" the hope to refer to possible objects of experience. Axinn (1994, esp. chapters 6, 7, and 8).

14 Kant, *Critique of Pure Reason*, A599/B626

15 Kant, *Critique of Practical Reason*, 5:143.

a license to rely on their truth, and the moral obligation to pursue the Highest Good as a decisive reason to do so.

So now we see a strong resemblance between hope, as conceived under the incorporation analysis, and the commitment Kant thinks we need to make to the practical postulates. Hope involves assigning a probability (0<p<1) to an outcome, and seeing that probability as licensing certain feelings and thoughts about that outcome, as well as hedged reliance on that outcome in one's plans. Committing to the practical postulates involves being theoretically agnostic about their truth, yet seeing their unprovable nature as licensing reliance on their truth in one's pursuit of the Highest Good. One notable difference is that hope also involves seeing the relevant probability as demanding a back-up plan, while committing to the practical postulates requires no such plan. So it might seem this commitment is more like an attitude of expectation than hope. However, the lack of demand for a back-up plan is due to the *practical* status of the postulates. They are *necessary* conditions for the achievement of a *necessary* end. A back-up plan is impossible, and one cannot rationally abandon the relevant end. In other words, when it comes to the practical postulates, practical need collapses the distinction between hope and expectation—at least as far as our plans are concerned. There might remain a difference in the associated thoughts and feelings. I'll set this issue aside, and simply conclude that, so far, it appears Kant is arguing for something very much like hope.

The Transformation of Hope into Faith

However, Kant's description of the upright man suggests one further element of the morally required commitment to the practical postulates. He says that the upright man refuses to "pay attention to rationalizations." The rationalizations he has in mind are no doubt theoretical challenges from the atheist. This suggests that commitment to the practical postulates requires being *confident* about one's position, believing no theoretical challenge could be adequate to undermine one's willingness to rely on them in one's endeavors. This kind of confidence is the mark of *faith*—Kant is arguing for (of course) moral faith. In a slogan: faith is hope plus confidence. More accurately and less concisely: faith is what you get when you add a certain meta-confidence to either hope or expectation—the confidence that you will never have theoretical reason to stop seeing the theoretical status of the relevant outcome as licensing hopeful or expectant thoughts, feelings, and plans.[16] When the

16 As noted above, it cannot be rationally legitimate to think about an unimaginable hope in the sense of imagining experiencing the hoped-for outcome, or fantasizing about it. It can, however, be legitimate to "think" the hope in a more abstract sense: see, for example, Axinn on reasonably

hopeful person is aware that she hopes for an inconceivable or unimaginable outcome and that her hope is therefore immune to disappointment in the ways discussed above, this confidence is legitimate. Kant's argument is (of course) an attempt to establish the *rational legitimacy* of moral faith.

Note that whether Kant's moral faith really is rationally legitimate in the way just described depends on the truth of the claim that there are no objectively sufficient grounds for believing or disbelieving (in the contemporary sense) the propositions that the immortal soul and God exist. Kant believed he had established this in the *Critique of Pure Reason*, and I will not attempt to raise doubts about it here. The point I aim to make through the examination of Kant on moral faith is that, if a person does form a hope that targets a genuinely unimaginable outcome, the possibility or impossibility of which cannot be established theoretically, then it is rationally legitimate for her to also take on board the meta-confidence I have called the mark of faith: the confidence that nothing she encounters can give her reason to stop hoping.

Plenty Coups' hope, it seems to me, is a good candidate for such a hope. As discussed above, this hope that the Crow would find a new way to flourish as Crow was unimaginable in the sense I have been describing: the Crow found themselves in a situation where they were unable to be Crow, to engage in the activities that defined them in their own eyes. So to hope for a new way to flourish was really that—to hope for an entirely *new* way of being that was nevertheless somehow still a way of being *Crow*. Plenty Coups' hope was also for an outcome that was, for him, unimaginably good. It relied on the belief that the good, too, outstripped his concepts. As Lear says, this hope "manifests a commitment to the idea that the goodness of the world transcends one's limited and vulnerable attempts to understand it."[17] That is, the outcome Plenty Coups hoped for outstripped his concepts, generally speaking, and more specifically outstripped his concept of a good life. His hope was such that it would always be rational for him to deny that any particular worldly outcome was its disappointment, or that any experience was evidence that the outcome for which he hoped was not good. Plenty Coups was thus justified in adopting the meta-confidence of faith, the attitude that no experience could provide reason for him to stop seeing the chances of his tribe surviving and flourishing as sufficient to license hopeful thoughts, feelings, and plans.

One might worry that this faith could not possibly be rational, because there was one development that surely even Plenty Coups could not have denied qualified as the disappointment of his hope: the annihilation of the Crow nation. Suppose his diplomatic efforts had entirely failed, and the white

---

mentioning a transcendental hope to oneself in thought, rather than unreasonably using the hope to refer to possible objects of experience: Axinn (1994, 223–28).

17   Lear, "*Radical Hope.*"

man had slaughtered the Crow, leaving Plenty Coups the last Crow standing. Would not Plenty Coups, perhaps as he lay on his death bed, then have to admit that his hope was in vain, and that the Crow did not and would not find a way to live well as Crow people? Plenty Coups could perhaps resist this conclusion by maintaining that *dying well* is a crucial element of living well, and hoping that the Crow had managed to die well. That is, he could resist admitting that his hope was vain if his hope was that the Crow could *do well with their situation*, and find a way to be Crow no matter what their circumstances. If they had no choice but to die, then his hope was that they had died well as Crow.

We see then, that in order for Plenty Coups' hope to be truly immune to disappointment it has to be refined a bit. The hope that the Crow would someday flourish as Crow has to be, at base, a hope focused on the Crow people's actions and not on the Crow people's situation at large. There is a form of flourishing that a person's circumstances can place out of reach: the world, or other people, can make it impossible for one to even approximate this form of flourishing by withholding sustenance needs, education, opportunities for creative development and social connections, and so on.[18] If it was this form of flourishing that Plenty Coups hoped his people would find, then his hope could not be entirely immune to disappointment, and so it could not be a rational faith (of the ilk I have identified—I don't mean to deny there are other conceptions of faith with a lower bar.) If, however, what Plenty Coups hoped was that his people would adapt to their situation as well as possible, finding flexible ways to continue to be Crow, he could rationally maintain the position I have described, and thus adopt a rational faith in his people.

The important distinction that Lear's example of Plenty Coups points up is that there are both outcomes that are *necessarily unimaginable* and outcomes that are only *contingently unimaginable*. Kant's hopes are for *necessarily unimaginable* outcomes: concepts of the divine are by definition (at least on his view) concepts that reach beyond possible experience and cognition. Plenty Coups' hope, by contrast, is for an outcome (survival as Crow) that he *may one day be able to experience*—indeed, it would be strange to think a people could survive without knowing it, so Plenty Coups' hope is for the Crow to find a way of life that they *will know* constitutes their survival as Crow. This outcome outstrips his present concepts, but not all possible experience. Similarly for the goodness of this outcome: the hope is that they will both

---

18   See Martha Nussbaum, "Human Functioning and Social Justice: In Defense of Aristotelian Essentialism," *Political Theory* 20.2 (1992): 202–46; Nussbaum, *Creating Capabilities: The Human Development Approach* (Cambridge, MA: Belknap Press of Harvard University Press, 2011); Amartya Sen, "Equality of What?" in *Liberty, Equality, and Law: Selected Tanner Lectures on Moral Philosophy*, John Rawls and Sterling M. McMurrin, eds. (Salt Lake City, UT: University of Utah Press, 1987); Sen, "Rights and Capabilities," *Resources, Values and Development* (Cambridge, MA: Harvard University Press, 1984), 307–24.

find a good Crow life and experience it as such. And this outcome outstrips his present concept of goodness, but not all possible experience of goodness. In other words, it is possible for hope to be unimaginable (and thus transformed into a faith that is immune to disappointment) and yet not target an immediately religious outcome. Nevertheless, as previously mentioned, Plenty Coups' hope/faith was in fact religious, based on trust in the goodness of *Ah-badt-dadt-deah* and his favor. So we might wonder whether unimaginable hope must target an outcome that, if not immediately religious, at least presupposes religious commitments. And this brings us to Marcel.

Marcel's Hope

Any discussion of what I am calling unimaginable hope and its connection to faith would be remiss if it did not include mention of the early-twentieth-century French philosopher and playwright, Gabriel Marcel. Marcel is an odd duck, philosophically speaking. He was arguably among the first existentialists, since at the heart of his philosophy is the idea that a personally unconnected or independent human existence is meaningless. Much of his work is also methodologically aligned with the phenomenological tradition, seeking to understand attitudes such as hope and despair through the examination of what it is like to experience them. And his work is also thoroughly Christian, to the point that it was labelled "Christian Existentialism" by Jean-Paul Sartre and others. His philosophical writing is quite diverse, and consciously unsystematic. However, a particular form of hope, both unimaginable (or, in Marcel's terminology "transcendent") and religious is a common theme in much of that writing. I will focus here on his lecture, "Sketch of a Phenomenology and Metaphysic of Hope."[19]

In this lecture, Marcel provides an account of the form of hope he thinks is essential to a meaningful existence and the possibility of human progress. He develops this account by contrasting this form of hope—I'll call it "Marcel's hope"—with the things it might be mistaken for but is not, and also by drawing conceptual and pragmatic connections between it and other feelings and attitudes. What I want to do here is present Marcel's hope in its full glory, so to speak, with all of the many features he attributes to it, and then peel away several of these features, in order to argue that not all are truly essential to the sustaining power of this form of hope. This will prepare us to consider the possibility of secular faith.

19 Gabriel Marcel, "Sketch of a Phenomenology and Metaphysic of Hope," in *Homo Viator: Introduction to a Metaphysic of Hope*, Emma Crawford, trans. (New York: Harper Torchbooks, 1962), 29–67. For a systematic account of Marcel's view of hope and its role in the ethical life, developed across a range of his works, see Jill Graper Hernandez, *Gabriel Marcel's Ethics of Hope: Evil, God and Virtue* (New York: Continuum Press, 2011).

Marcel's hope is never mundane—he defines it as arising in the context of a "trial." His principal examples of trials are illness, separation, exile, slavery, prolonged creative infertility, and the loss of a loved one.[20] He characterizes trials phenomenologically, and connects them with feelings of captivity and alienation. At the heart of this characterization is that a trial "invariably impl[ies] the impossibility . . . of rising to a certain fullness of life."[21] Illness may promise chronic fatigue and pain, the death of a loved one ongoing grief, writer's block permanent loss of creativity—each trial thereby threatens that one will never be able to pursue the projects that make up one's identity.

Marcel considers three possible responses to a trial: *despair, acceptance,* and *hope.* Each response is, at its heart, a shift in the trial sufferer's self-conception. A trial promises to prevent one from ever flourishing as one aspires. To *despair* is to embrace this promise, "to renounce the idea of remaining oneself[;] it is to be fascinated by the idea of one own destruction to the point of anticipating this very destruction itself."[22] On Marcel's view, any embrace of one's own destruction—such as suicide—is an act of despair. In order to clearly distinguish Marcel's sense of despair from the sense discussed in earlier chapters, I will call this "existential despair"—it is, essentially, to see one's destruction as the only way out of one's trial.[23]

To *accept* one's trial is, by contrast, to commit to keeping hold of oneself despite the inescapability of the trial and the limitations it imposes: "I do not consent . . . to be the useless creature which my illness or captivity may finally make of me; I will counter [the] fascination . . . this creature might have for me with the firm determination to remain what I am."[24] This "acceptance" is therefore in one sense not acceptance at all. That is, the person who accepts her trial, as Marcel characterizes her, does not "accept" the trial's promise to bring her low or permanently limit her ability to flourish. To the contrary, Marcel says she has a "firm determination" not to be destroyed by her trial.

---

20 Marcel, "Sketch of a Phenomenology and Metaphysic of Hope," 30, 65.

21 Ibid., 30.

22 Ibid., 37–38.

23 A sidenote: Marcel assumes that existential despair is essentially bad, worthy of condemnation. And his condemnation of suicide and the attitudes that lead to it is, like many Christian philosophers', too sweeping. For example, it would be strange to insist that Jim Witcher's attitude toward suicide is essentially bad. For one thing, attending to the fact that he can end his descent into death by paralysis eases his mind, gives him a sense of control, and makes it easier for him to abide his trial. Note, too, that suicide need not be self-*destruction*. Suicide is sometimes the only way of preserving oneself, as when one faces a disease like ALS, or the certainty that one will betray one's values in the course of a trial. So Marcel is mistaken, and not every case of seeing suicide in a hopeful way is a bad thing. Given this, demonstrating that an attitude is inconsistent with existential despair is not demonstrating that the attitude is intrinsically good or virtuous. Virtue is simply more context-sensitive than that. I will, however, set this complexity aside for the rest of the chapter, and focus on cases of existential despair where that attitude is mistaken or bad—where suicide is *not* the best way for a person to escape her trial, and/or it does not give her the strength to abide her trial.

24 Marcel, "Sketch of a Phenomenology and Metaphysic of Hope," 38.

Nevertheless, there is some sense in which she continues to see the trial as inescapable. Marcel associates acceptance with Stoicism, so we might think of it as the determination to persevere in spite of an acknowledged bad fate, along with the strategy of affective and desiderative detachment from that fate. Acceptance is thus literally inconsistent with existential despair, because it rules out embracing one's destruction as an escape from the trial.[25]

Finally, Marcel's *hope* is inconsistent with existential despair in a different way. Marcel first contrasts hope with acceptance by describing hope as "a non-acceptance, but positive and hence distinguishable from revolt."[26] But he goes on to say the following: "Hope means first accepting the trial as an integral part of the self, but while doing so it considers it as destined to be absorbed and transmuted by the inner workings of a certain creative process."[27] So the crucial difference between "acceptance" and hope is really the way in which one accepts the trial. Acceptance means taking the trial as a permanent condition and adapting oneself to live well within the limitations it imposes by eliminating the desire to escape it. Hope means taking the trial as a real but temporary condition, and adapting oneself to wait until it is "absorbed and transmuted"; one does not work to bring about this change, or even anticipate it, because one sees it as "destined." Hope is inconsistent with existential despair not because one no longer desires the end of the trial—for one does—but because seeing the trial as destined to end precludes seeing one's self-destruction as the only way to end it.

One might wonder why Marcel thinks it is necessary to see a trial as *destined* to end in order to fend off existential despair. After all, to oppose existential despair, even in the very robust sense of occupying the conceptual space this condition needs to exist, hope need only be for a certain kind of outcome: it suffices that hope is for the trial to end through some means inconsistent with one's destruction. It could be hope for one's own success in battling one's trial; it could be hope for a miracle cure; or it could be hope for aid from an unexpected source. So why the insistence on seeing the end of the trial as "destined"?

The answer is that Marcel is looking for a response to a trial that not only opposes existential despair, but also cannot be undermined by worldly events. He writes:

> [I]nsofar as I make my hope conditional I myself put limits to the process by which I could triumph over successive disappointments. . . . We can, on

---

25 There is one circumstance where acceptance does not seem to be inconsistent with suicide: where one's trial is an obstacle to committing suicide in a way that one values. For example, there are times in *A Death of One's Own* when Jim Witcher seems most agonized by the fear that he will wait too long and be unable to commit suicide by his own hand.

26 Marcel, "Sketch of a Phenomenology and Metaphysic of Hope," 38.

27 Ibid., 39.

the other hand, conceive, at least theoretically, of the inner disposition of one who, setting no condition or limit and abandoning himself in absolute confidence, would thus transcend all possible disappointment and would experience a security of his being.[28]

To make hope "conditional," in this context, is to hope for an outcome with *worldly* conditions, to have a hope that can be disappointed if worldly events fail to unfold as hoped. It is easy to see that such a hope, a hope with an expiration date, is vulnerable to being dashed. Marcel's example is hoping to recover from an illness by a certain date—when that date comes and goes, and the hopeful person still ails, her hope crumbles and potentially opens up space for existential despair to move in. The hope that she will recover, *eventually*, makes her less vulnerable but not immune to disappointment. It can, in other words, encounter a worldly condition that will force it to give way, leaving room for existential despair. Ultimately, I am going to argue that Marcel is mistaken. In fact, *no* unimaginable hope or faith is vulnerable as Marcel indicates—not even a merely contingently unimaginable hope, and not even a hope without religious inspiration. First, though, we should consider the other distinguishing features of Marcel's hope.

Grounding Hope in Love

At various points in the lecture, Marcel says the hope that sustains us through trials is *patient*, involves *trust* and *humility*, is grounded in *love*, and is "essentially distinct from the calculating faculty of reason."[29] Why, precisely, it has these exact marks is not immediately obvious. I think, however, that it is the last of them—the need Marcel perceives to separate hope from reason—that best explains the others. Specifically, he thinks that, if hope is grounded in love, it is able to meet this need, and that hope grounded in love, especially the love of God, is patient and humble. Let's see how this goes.

Near the end of the lecture, Marcel asks whether hoping is legitimate "when the reasons for so doing are insufficient or even completely lacking?" He frames the same query as the question of when one has a "right" to hope.[30] But he quickly reveals his assumption that the only reasons that could possibly bear on hope are considerations about the probability of the hoped-for outcome: the question, he writes, "springs from a calculating faculty of reason which, with the very approximate means at its disposal proceeds to carry out a regular balancing up of chances."[31] This, he claims, shows that

28   Ibid., 46.
29   Ibid., 46.
30   Ibid., 63.
31   Ibid., 64–65.

the question misconstrues the nature of hope. His motivation seems to be the reasonable presupposition that hoping against hope—hoping in the face of acknowledged low probabilities—*has* to be legitimate, at least sometimes; and, of course, if the only reasons that bear on hope regard the probability of the hoped-for outcome, then one has very little reason to hope for low-probability outcomes. It is thus easy enough to see why Marcel thinks hope must be "essentially distinct from reason."

Now of course I have argued that hope is *not* essentially distinct from reason, that it is governed by norms of practical as well as theoretical rationality, and that it is possible to satisfy these norms even when hoping for a very low-probability outcome. So I disagree with Marcel's starting point, that hope must be essentially distinct from reason. If, however, I held his rather Humean view of reason, according to which it is merely a calculating faculty, I would agree. So I'll set aside this point and proceed to the rest of his view.

How can hope be beyond reason's purview? That, according to Marcel, is where love comes in. He provides the following case:

> Take, for instance, a mother who persists in hoping that she will see her son again although his death has been certified in the most definite manner by witnesses who found his body, buried it, etc. Is not the observer justified in saying that there are no reasons for hoping that this son is still alive? . . . [W]e have the right to say: "No, objectively speaking, the return must be considered as impossible." But at the root of the mother's objective judgment . . . she has written within her a loving thought which repudiates or transcends the facts, and it seems as though there was something absurd or even scandalous in disputing her right to hope, that is to say to love, against all hope. More exactly, what is absurd is the very idea of a right which we can recognize or dispute.[32]

If hope is an expression of love, he suggests, then at least from the point of view of the experiencing subject, it is inappropriate to hold it to norms of rationality. This is true even if there is sufficient reason to believe the hoped-for outcome is *certain* not to occur. Why should this be? I think Phillip Stratton-Lake is right when he says Marcel relies on a conception of love that exploits our reluctance to identify reasons for loving the people we do.[33] The idea is that, if love is an arational attitude (or loving an arational activity), then expressions of love are similarly arational.

This brings us to patience, trust, and humility. The mere grounding of hope in love for another person does not directly entail these attitudes. Hoping for, or on behalf of, or for the sake of something valued by one's beloved,

32 Ibid., 65.

33 Philip Stratton-Lake, "Marcel, Hope and Virtue," in *French Existentialism: Consciousness, Ethics and Relations with Others*, James Giles, ed. (Amsterdam: Rodolphi, 1999).

doesn't necessarily commit one to the kind of surrender and vulnerability to the beloved implicit in patience, trust, and humility. That is, such a grounding of hope in love doesn't imply these attitudes, *unless love itself is the right kind of surrender*. And that is exactly the case, if the mother's love for her son is a specification of her love for God. As Marcel says:

> This is what determines the ontological position of hope—absolute hope, inseparable from a faith which is likewise absolute, transcending all laying down of conditions, and for this very reason every kind of representation whatever it might be. The only possible source from which this absolute hope springs must once more be stressed. It appears as a response of the creature to the infinite Being to whom it is conscious of owing everything that it has and upon whom it cannot impose any condition whatsoever without scandal.[34]

For Marcel, all these things are of a piece: the hope for communion with God, loving-trusting hope, the hope of humility and surrender, patient hope, hope that transcends the norms of rationality, unimaginable hope (as I have called it). This is the hope that not only protects us from falling into existential despair, but is truly ironclad, invulnerable to disappointment by experience. This kind of hope, he thinks, must be "inseparable from" religious faith. In other words, according to Marcel, the form of hope that has special value and philosophical interest, and that intrinsically opposes existential despair, is in fact faith that one will find communion with God, who through divine beneficence will resolve one's trial in the best possible way—a way one is not yet equipped to understand or anticipate in any detail.

Marcel's hope is doubtless a powerful source of sustenance in the face of even the most debilitating trials. Moreover, Plenty Coups' hope seems at least a close kin to Marcel's. It seems like a loving hope placed in and on behalf of his people, and it has the religious origins to imbue it with the elements of patience, trust, and humility that Marcel says mark "absolute hope." The primary difference is that Plenty Coups' hope is, as I argued before, for a *contingently* unimaginable outcome, rather than for something that transcends "every kind of representation whatever it might be." I have also suggested, however, that even this contingently unimaginable hope can develop an immunity to disappointment, if it is framed as a hope that the Crow find a way to do well as Crow, come what may, even in death. So I have no wish to cast doubt on Marcel's conception of hope in this regard.

Nevertheless, I do want to challenge the idea that hope *must* have *all* of these features to be such a powerful source of sustenance. For Marcel's hope is available to quite a limited group: those for whom the belief in a Christian God infuses human relations. This is a much smaller set of people than those

---

34 Marcel, "Sketch of a Phenomenology and a Metaphysic of Hope," 46–47.

who believe in a Divine Authority or Creator, or even those who believe in an Infinite Being of the sort Marcel describes. Thus, I want now to bring to bear on Marcel's and Plenty Coups' hopes an analysis of unimaginable hope or faith drawn from Kant, in order to argue for the possibility of a secular faith with the same sustaining power.

The Possibility of Secular Faith

Let me begin by raising some concerns about the importance Marcel assigns to love. This is not to suggest that I don't think loving hope is a wonderful and valuable part of human experience—I want only to consider the view that even hope arising from love is governed by rational norms and argue that this view is not "scandalous," as Marcel suggests. So, let us return to the mother's hope to see her dead son again.

Contrary to Marcel and Stratton-Lake, I don't think love and loving are entirely arational. I think loving someone consists in, first, having subrational attractions to and with regard to her and, second, incorporating those attractions into one's agency by treating them as reasons for adopting certain ends. That is, I think that love has a structure much like hope's as it appears under the incorporation analysis, and that it is partly governed by norms of practical rationality.[35] However, I agree with Marcel that the mother's hope to see her beloved child might very well be the expression of an arational element of her love, because one constituent of her love might be a representation of him walking through the door as incredibly attractive or compelling. Still, her hope does not consist entirely in this attraction and, on the incorporation analysis, the certainty that her child is dead does indeed render her hope rationally tenuous, if not outright irrational. If she maintains hope by deceiving herself about the possibility that her son is still alive, then she is epistemically irrational. If she is clear-eyed about this impossibility, but manages to adopt the hopeful licensing stance toward it nonetheless, then she is likely practically irrational: she is unlikely to advance her rational ends by relying on an outcome she knows is certain not to obtain. And of course, spending emotional and mental energy on the possibility of his return is likely not to advance her rational ends.

So I am fairly committed to seeing the mother's hope as irrational. I am not, however, committed to seeing her *love* as irrational—my view entails only that there are irrational ways of expressing this love. Rationally speaking, she would be better off expressing her love through hopes that do not rely on deceiving herself about the facts or treating the facts as licensing self-defeating behavior. Marcel thinks such a view is "scandalous." But where is

---

35   Martin ms, "Love and Agency," (ms).

the scandal in simply recognizing irrationality? As long as the mother's hope that her son is still alive consoles her and does not hurt her or others in any serious way, it would be cruel and pointless to force rationality on her—we have a "right" to be irrational, in some circumstances.

Thus, a loving hope is no more arational than other forms of hope, and there is no reason to shy away from this fact. Yet one still might think hope has to be religious in some sense if it is to provide the noncontingent sustenance of Marcel's and Plenty Coups' hopes. Consider, however, this passage from Lear:

> We do not have to agree with Plato that there is a transcendent source of goodness—that is, a source of goodness that transcends the world—to think that the goodness *of the world* transcends our finite powers to grasp it. . . . And this is the core of Plenty Coups' commitment. His specifically religious beliefs were crucially important to him, but in my opinion, they gave him the sustenance with which he could hold onto this core commitment through the storm. The core commitment itself can be held by the secular and the religious; it is an appropriate response to our being finite natures.[36]

There are two points I want to make about this passage. First, I want to offer further support for Lear's claim that secular unimaginable hope is possible—that is, hope for an outcome whose nature and goodness outstrip the hopeful person's concepts. Second, I want to show that, even if it is true that Plenty Coups' religious beliefs "gave him the sustenance with which he could hold onto" his hope, sustenance in the form of the confidence of the faithful, at least, does not presuppose religious beliefs.

On the first point, one might think there is at least something *quasi-religious* about Plenty Coups' "core commitment," in that it appears to make goodness metaphysically independent of us—it seems to require that there is goodness in the world to be discovered by us. Such robust realism is likely to rub naturalists of a certain stripe the wrong way. I think, however, that the concept of worldly but transcendent goodness does not in fact require such robust realism. It is enough that it is possible for us to encounter situations requiring what Barbara Herman has called "moral improvisation."[37]

A situation requires moral improvisation when a shift in social, cultural, political, or even natural circumstances renders familiar moral categories irrelevant, or known ways of applying those categories ineffective. Herman's example is in post-apartheid South Africa. She argues that standard or familiar concepts of political justice were a bad fit for the situation: holding

---

36 Lear, *Radical Hope*, 121–22.
37 Barbara Herman, "Moral Improvisation," *Moral Literacy* (Cambridge, MA: Harvard University Press, 2008).

ordinary citizens responsible and enacting retributive justice upon them would fail to fully recognize the *systematic* injustice that was Apartheid. Nelson Mandela's moral improvisation was the Truth and Reconciliation Commission, where both the victims and perpetrators of Apartheid made their stories part of the public record—the aim being to enact a new sort of justice, one more adequate to the nature of Apartheid's wrong. Even if one objects to the Truth and Reconciliation Commission's forgoing retributive justice, Herman and others make a compelling case that the public narrative constituted its own distinct form of justice, tailored to the situation.[38]

The Crow people were in a situation requiring the ultimate moral improvisation. Lear argues that they needed to "thin" the virtues—the constituents of a good life—in order to de-particularize them. They needed, for example, a version of courage that was not tied to military conquest. Nelson Mandela's strategy, on Herman's interpretation, was the same, although she does not describe it as "thinning" a moral concept, but rather as figuring out a new way to respond to a more general value (justice) underwriting a specific value inadequate to the situation (retributive justice). The Stoic Seneca, too, discusses this process: when a principle clearly fails to produce the right policy in a given situation, he argues, we should go back, recall the original purpose of the principle, and modify it to serve that purpose in the new situation.

Thus, I think Lear is right when he points out that believing the good can transcend one's comprehension of it does not imply any religious or supernatural commitments. Another way to see this point is to ask what Plenty Coups' hope would have lost, if he had not been a religious man. He could still have seen his vision as a kind of insight—the kind of insight I previously argued fantasy sometimes provides—though not a vision given to him by anyone or anything other than his own mind. He could still have formed the hope that the Crow would find a new way to flourish as Crow. In other words, he could have hoped the Crow would succeed in an extreme form of moral improvisation. His hope would have targeted an outcome conceived as "thinly" good, or under the general value "a good life." And this brings us to confidence.

I argued earlier that, when hope targets an unimaginable outcome, the hopeful person is in a position to adopt a certain meta-confidence, defined as a confidence that nothing she experiences will give her reason to abandon her hope. And that is what we see here. Given the thinness or generality of Plenty Coups' conception of the hoped-for outcome, it would have been rational for him to deny any development counted as disappointing his hope. And, if he had been aware of the (contingently) unimaginable nature of his hope, it would have been rational for him to adopt the meta-confidence of faith, even absent any religious beliefs. This would have been a secular faith.

38 Ibid., 320.

Summary

There are many ways of committing suicide, some literal, some figurative. The temptation our greatest trials present is the idea that suicide of one form or another might be the best way to evade being crushed: physically, emotionally, spiritually, evaluatively. I have argued that there are many kinds of hope that counter this idea, that can occupy the conceptual space existential despair requires to exist. I have also argued that there is a more rarified form of hope that is not only a conceptual counter to existential despair, but also a way of lifting oneself out of the world of experience and pinning one's sights on an outcome that one is always justified in hoping for. This unimaginable hope is a plausible candidate for the attitude we call "faith," and under certain conditions it is a rational form of confidence in the possibility of a good outcome to a trial. The hope I discussed in chapter 3 has a contingent sustaining power, but faith is essentially sustaining.

In the next, and final, chapter, I change tracks. Until now, I have focused primarily on hopes regarding events that are not necessarily exercises of agency. As I hinted toward the end of chapter 1, however, I believe there is a class of hopes that are distinct in an important way—the hopes we place *in* people. When we place hope in a person, we commit ourselves to an interesting conception of her as a free and rational agent. This conception, I will argue, is not exactly the same as the conception implied when we hold people fully responsible for their actions; it is, instead, a way of aspiring *for* people that they become fully free and responsible, while acknowledging the challenges posed by both external and internal obstacles.

Normative Hope

In this chapter, I turn to the way we sometimes place hope *in* people, and argue that it is a distinctive and fundamental way of relating to people *interpersonally*. Normatively hoping for a person to live up to some principle of behavior is a way of aspiring on her behalf, which is closely related to but different from holding her responsible for her behavior. I begin, therefore, with Strawson, and the idea that we hold people responsible by adopting certain "reactive" feelings or attitudes.

Strawson and the Reactive Attitudes

In his classic 1969 paper, "Freedom and Resentment," Peter Strawson argues that the question whether we are free and responsible agents is a practical question that cannot be answered by theoretical propositions like determinism. His argument is that a valuable and natural mode of human interaction essentially involves "reactive" attitudes or feelings, which presuppose that their targets are free and responsible agents. Abandoning our commitment to a person's freedom and responsibility requires abandoning this mode of interaction; we can and do abandon it on local occasions and with regard to local individuals but, Strawson argues, to do so globally would be undesirable, irrational, and even psychologically impossible.[1] His argument has of course been challenged in a variety of ways, but it is nevertheless fair to say that in its general spirit it has been more widely and thoroughly embraced than most arguments. Indeed, "Freedom and Resentment" has generated an entire branch of moral psychology dedicated to examining the reactive attitudes and their role in our practices of holding each other and ourselves responsible.

Jonathan Bennett argues that it is impossible to define the reactive attitudes, and that the best we can do is list exemplars: resentment, indignation,

---

1 Strawson, "Freedom and Resentment."

guilt, pride, gratitude, admiration, etc.[2] He is probably right about the first; it is not possible to give a *reductive* definition of the reactive attitudes whereby we analyze them into elements not themselves conceptually tied to our practices of holding people responsible, or treating people as free and responsible agents. About the second, however, he is mistaken. We can learn a good deal about the reactive attitudes and their function by drawing out the connections between them and concepts like *holding responsible* and *interpersonal relations*, and so on. Each of these concepts is in turn tied back to the reactive attitudes, but the circle here is virtuous, informative so long as we do not attempt to treat any of its links as a reductive definition.

A number of philosophers have followed the virtuous circle line of thought. One of the most fruitful efforts has been to follow up on Strawson's suggestion that the reactive attitudes are expressions of a "basic demand" for good will from those with whom we interact. As Bennett points out, this is no good as a reductive definition:

[I]f it has any explanatory value, it runs the other way, enabling us to explain "demand" by reference to indignation, as Strawson does: "the making of the demand *is* the proneness to such attitudes . . ."[3]

However, as philosophers like Gary Watson, Jay Wallace, and Stephen Darwall have argued, the "explanatory value" of such claims is not limited to the provision of reductive definitions.[4] When we discover that to demand good will from someone is to be prone to indignation in certain circumstances, and vice versa, we learn about the psychological function of both the demand and the feeling of indignation. We also learn about the justification conditions for both the demand and the feeling.[5]

However, Bennett makes two further points that require refinements to this and similar claims. First, the reactive attitudes are not always responses to failures of good *will*; we can, for example, be indignant about someone's attitude toward natural beauty.[6] Wallace's account of holding people responsible is a good example of how to accommodate this point. He characterizes the

2 Jonathan Bennett, "Accountability," in *Philosophical Subjects: Essays Presented to P. F. Strawson*, Zak van Straaten, ed. (Oxford: Clarendon Press, 1980).

3 Ibid., 42.

4 See Stephen Darwall; Watson, *Agency and Answerability: Selected Essays* (Oxford and New York: Oxford University Press, 2009); and Wallace, *Responsibility and the Moral Sentiments*.

5 Further important discussions of Strawson and the participant stance include Fischer and Ravizza, *Responsibility and Control* (Cambridge: Cambridge University Press, 1998); Coleen Macnamara, "Holding Others Responsible," *Philosophical Studies* 152 (2011): 81–102; T. M. Scanlon, *Moral Dimensions: Permissibility, Meaning, Blame* (Cambridge: Cambridge University Press, 2008); Angela Smith, "On Being Responsible and Holding Responsible," *Journal of Ethics* 11.4 (2007), 465–84; Susan Wolf, "The Importance of Free Will," *Mind* 90 (1981): 386–405; Wolf, *Freedom within Reason* (Oxford: Oxford University Press, 1990).

6 Bennett, "Accountability," 45–46.

reactive attitudes as those attitudes that presuppose holding their target to a "normative expectation"—this expectation could be that one display the right attitude toward other people, but it could also be that one display the right attitude toward, say, natural beauty. Practical requirements can apply to interpersonal attitudes, intrapersonal attitudes, attitudes toward things other than people, perhaps even behaviors independent of attitude; and we can "normatively expect" or demand people to conform to any of these requirements.[7]

Bennett's second point about theorizing the reactive attitudes via their relation to demands or normative expectations is that it narrows the class of reactive attitudes to exclude many of the attitudes Strawson first identifies as reactive: "I doubt if 'demand' really covers all the ground: I can find no place for it in describing such undisappointed reactive feelings as those of gratitude and reciprocating love."[8] Wallace embraces this point and attributes Strawson's inclusion of attitudes not essentially connected with normative expectation—"such attitudes as embarrassment, friendly affection, and sympathy"[9]—to a tendency to conflate the so-called "participant" attitudes with the reactive attitudes. Strawson uses the label "participant" for any attitude that is involved in or points us to "normal interpersonal relations"—an elusive notion we will come to shortly. And, as Wallace points out, Strawson and many who have followed him have assumed that the reactive attitudes—those constitutive of our practices of holding people responsible—are to be identified with the participant attitudes. Insofar as we are interested in these practices, however, Wallace rightly argues we should recognize that

> The reactive attitudes are not co-extensive with the emotions one feels toward people with whom one has interpersonal relationships, rather they constitute a particular category of emotion specially distinguished by its constitutive connection with expectations.[10]

The central reactive attitudes are, he says, resentment, indignation, and guilt. It is tempting to think he may have narrowed the field too far, and certain positive feelings like gratitude are conceptually connected to normative expectation: namely, gratitude, admiration, and pride, which seem like feelings that mark when a person has exceeded a norm to which one holds her (within the limits set by other normative expectations). I will argue, however, that Wallace is right to treat asymmetrically cases of failing and meeting (or exceeding) normative expectations. Gratitude—along with admiration and pride—is not conceptually connected with normative expectation in the

7   For example, Wallace gives examples of normative expectations such as "Do not break the promise you made to your sister," which seem to dictate behavior and not attitude. Wallace, *Responsibility and the Moral Sentiments*, 22.

8   Bennett, "Accountability," 42.

9   Wallace, *Responsibility and the Moral Sentiments*, 27.

10   Ibid., 31.

same way as resentment, indignation, and guilt. Instead, these positive emotions are manifestations of a closely related but importantly distinct stance I will call "normative hope." Before I can make this argument, however, we need a picture of the broader practice within which normative expectation or holding responsible sits.

The idea I want pursue is that holding people to normative expectations and being prone to the reactive attitudes, narrowly construed, is *one way* to relate to people *interpersonally*, or from the "participant" stance. In the end, I want to argue that certain hopes constitute another, closely related form of interpersonal engagement. To see this, we need to better understand this idea, *interpersonal engagement*.

Mapping the Territory: Interpersonal Relations

Engaging with someone interpersonally stands in contrast with taking what Strawson calls an "objective" attitude toward her:

> To adopt the objective attitude toward another human being is to see him, perhaps, as an object of social policy; as a subject for what, in a whole range of senses, might be called treatment; as something certainly to be taken account, perhaps precautionary account, of; to be managed or handled or cured or trained; perhaps simply to be avoided . . . The objective attitude may be emotionally toned in many ways, but not in all ways: it may include repulsion or fear, it may include pity or even love, though not all kinds of love. But it cannot include the range of . . . feelings and attitudes which belong to involvement or participation with others in interpersonal human relationships.[11]

This and the surrounding remarks on the objective attitude are more suggestive than anything else, and Bennett also despairs of defining either the objective attitude or the purportedly contrastive form of interpersonal engagement. He raises the therapist-patient relation, especially the therapist's relation to the patient, as a problem case:

> A therapist and his patient can be closely *involved* with one another, in a therapeutic programme in which they both *participate*; but that involvement might be quite untouched by anything Strawson would call 'reactive', at least on the therapist's side. . . . The intention to exclude therapist-patient working relationships is clear, but they are not being excluded by anything with which one could build a theory. . . . As for 'interpersonal relationships': well, the therapist is one person and his patient is another;

---

11 Strawson, "Freedom and Resentment," 9–10.

and if they do not have what 'we normally understand' by an interpersonal relationship then what we normally understand must be narrow. The narrowing may be well founded, but until we can say what it rests on we cannot avail ourselves of it. The job cannot be done with any formula about a relation in which each party treats the other as a person; for the therapist does treat his patient as a person—a person who needs help.[12]

The therapist adopts an attitude toward her patient whereby she is not disposed to feel a certain class of emotions toward him—she is not prepared to (more, she actively prepares herself not to) resent it when he is a jerk to her, to be angered by his mistreatment of others, and so on. So, if interpersonal engagement is marked by the disposition to feel such reactive attitudes, she is not relating to him *interpersonally*. But, Bennett objects, what, other than this resistance to the reactive attitudes, marks her attitude as "objective" rather than "interpersonal"? She is a person, her patient is a person, and they interact.

Now, we might simply continue the virtuous circle approach and insist we don't need anything other than the therapist's resistance to the reactive attitudes to mark off this relation as "objective." I think, though, the lesson we should take is that Wallace is right: insofar as we take resentment as the paradigm exemplar of the reactive attitudes, and our interest in these attitudes stems from a desire to understand our practices of holding responsible, relating to someone interpersonally and being disposed to the reactive attitudes are not the same thing. Being disposed to the reactive attitudes is holding someone responsible, and holding someone responsible is only one way of relating to her "interpersonally." Another is to be her therapist, to see her as a person who needs help. That is, we need to revise Strawson's account, both insofar as he identifies the reactive attitudes and all interpersonal attitudes, and insofar as he means to exclude (all) therapist-patient relations from the realm of interpersonal relations.

What is it to relate to someone interpersonally, if it is not necessarily to hold her responsible? It is, I submit, to relate to her as a reasoner. To relate to someone as a reasoner is not just to treat her in a way that relies on her capacity to reason, but also to stand ready to *exchange* reasons with her, to give and take reasons for belief, thought, action, etc. To take an objective attitude toward someone is, by contrast, to refuse or resist this kind of exchange, or to think it impossible. As Strawson says, "If your attitude toward someone is wholly objective, then . . . though you may talk to him, even negotiate with him, *you cannot reason with him*."[13]

This, then, is the map I am sketching. When we relate to someone *interpersonally*, we treat her as a reasoner. We stand ready to offer her reasons—not just carrots and sticks—for acting, believing, and so on. There are many ways

---

12   Bennett, "Accountability," 35–36.
13   Strawson, "Freedom and Resentment," 10 (emphasis added).

to be prepared to enter into an exchange of reasons with a person. One way is to *hold her to norms*, to normatively expect or demand that she regulate her behavior according to certain requirements and prohibitions. Here, the reasons of interest are the reasons one believes she has to conform to these norms—and these could include the intrinsic or extrinsic value of conformity, as well as the fact that one normatively expects conformity. For example, the parent who catches his teenage child in a lie may accuse her of both violating a general moral obligation and failing him on a personal level.[14] This parent offers these moral and personal considerations as reasons—he encourages her to take them up into her deliberation and treat them as reasons for feeling guilty about her behavior and adopting a policy of honesty.

The reactive attitudes, as I will now reserve the label, are the feelings conceptually tied to this specific way of treating someone as a reasoner. To normatively expect a person to conform to a norm is to be disposed to feel resentment, indignation, or guilt. These feelings all have the same base note, because they all presuppose holding someone to a norm. Guilt, of course, is distinguished by being *self*-reactive. It presupposes that the agent holds herself to norms. The other primary distinction, between resentment and indignation, is due to the fact that there are different ways to hold a person to a norm. As Darwall argues, resentment presupposes that one holds the violator *personally* accountable. If the parent *resents* his child's lie, that reveals that he sees her as owing honesty *to him*; he believes she has what has become known as a "bipolar obligation." If he feels indignation, that reveals that he sees her as impersonally obligated, or as owing honesty to the moral community at large. Darwall ties these different modes of holding accountable to different forms of authority. The resentful father alleges he has "individual authority." This is the authority to claim a special right to his daughter's honesty, a right he has in virtue of their particular relationship. The indignant father alleges "representative authority." This is authority he has to claim as a representative of the moral community; she has the implied obligation in virtue of her membership in this community, rather than in virtue of any special relationships she has to particular members of this community.[15] If he is both indignant and resentful, that indicates he holds his daughter both impersonally and personally accountable—the reasons he offers her, both for why she should have been honest and for why his angry feelings are warranted—include both the general obligation to be honest and the specific obligation she has to him. Wallace has a similar view, except that he ties "vicarious" attitudes like resentment not to representation of the moral community at large, but rather to a particular individual or group.[16] The most important point, for my purposes,

---

14 Not to say that the latter is necessarily a nonmoral obligation.

15 Darwall, "Bipolar Obligations" (ms).

16 Jay Wallace, "Emotions and Relationships: On a Strawsonian Theme" (ms).

is that resentment and indignation are twin feelings, in a manner of speaking: they are responses to the same kind of behavior—behavior against which someone has a *claim*—but on behalf of different parties.

Now, it would not be surprising if the father did not exactly feel resentment or indignation. The more standard feeling in this sort of scenario is *disappointment*, a feeling of having been *let down*. That is because we do not always *hold* our teenage children to norms in the same way we do competent adults. Especially when we recognize that conforming to a norm is very difficult for our children, we instead practice subtle scaffolding. We treat them as responsible agents . . . but not quite. We are thereby disposed to feel a set of feelings closely related to the reactive attitudes. This way of relating to a person is, I will argue, best theorized as a form of hope. Before we come to that, however, we should quickly re-traverse the borders of interpersonal relations outside of holding people responsible.

Holding a person responsible is just one way of treating her as a reasoner—that is, of being prepared to reason with her. There are so many different ways of relating to someone as a reasoner that it would be fruitless to venture a taxonomy. One can relate to someone as a reasoner by being prepared to deliberate *with* her, as in a shared project; by sharing appreciation with her for something beautiful or creative or unusual (or, to borrow Bennett's example, by becoming irritated with her failure to appreciate something beautiful[17]); by trusting her to follow basic coordination strategies like the rules of the road; and on and on. Many of the feelings that Strawson mentions in association with the core reactive attitudes and that Bennett rightly observes have no deep connection with demanding conformity to a norm appear somewhere in this territory. Call these feelings, such as hurt feelings and adult reciprocal love, "interpersonal feelings."

The therapist-patient relationship that both Bennett and Wallace consider such a challenge for Strawson also lands in this territory, inside interpersonal relations and outside holding responsible. We should begin by noting that this case is difficult to categorize in part because it is underdescribed. There are all sorts of therapies, and some probably do allow the therapist to hold her patients responsible in the way we have been discussing. Others are highly "objective," and the therapist tries to take an almost mechanistic view of her patients so as to condition them out of self-sabotaging habits. Most forms of therapy lie somewhere in between, allowing the therapist to feel sympathy, affection, and pride in relation to her patients, but not resentment or indignation. The cases that are supposed be a problem for Strawson are those where the therapist forswears the reactive attitudes but still should plausibly be interpreted as relating to her patients as persons.

As I have mapped the relevant territory, such a case is not at all perplexing. The therapeutic project, as this therapist conceives it, requires staying away

---

17 I do disagree with Bennett with regard to the possibility of unprincipled resentment.

from the reactive attitudes—helping her patients requires giving them a safe space where they can work through their fears, obsessions, and so on, without risking normative condemnation. But, except for the extreme case of the trainer-therapist, this project also requires continuing to relate to her patients as reasoners, sharing and exchanging reasons with them—especially reasons relevant to their shared project of helping the patient function better in the world. Even the trainer-therapist likely engages in this latter shared deliberation, at least if part of her project is to teach her patients how to "self-train."

This, then, is the mark of an interpersonal relation: the readiness to share or exchange reasons with somebody. As mentioned previously, it is not enough to merely make use of the fact that someone is a reasoner; one must sincerely interact with her *as* a reasoner. The difference between "making use" and "sincerely interacting" is subtle, and not one I can defend or analyze. There is a difference, however, between deliberating with a friend about what movie to see and running through exactly the same conversation with the intent of manipulating her to see the movie one wants to see.[18] Perhaps Kantians are right, and the difference needs to be understood in terms of rational consent—that is, the person to whom one relates interpersonally can rationally consent to one's influences on her reasoning and choices. Something along these lines does seem a plausible link in the circle of concepts containing "interpersonal relations," "interpersonal attitudes," "relating to as a reasoner," and so on.

The specific kind of interpersonal relation I want to focus on here is, as I indicated earlier, a close sibling of holding responsible, or normatively expecting conformity to a principle. I will call this sibling "normatively hoping" for conformity to a principle. I am going to elucidate normative hope first by introducing a puzzle about gratitude, and then returning to the case of the parent's disappointment in an errant child.

Gratitude, Disappointment, and Normative Hope

The first, rather obvious point to make is that "there is one way of [hoping for] a thing to happen that does not have any special connection with morality, or with moral emotions."[19] Wallace makes this point with regard to expectation, remarking that, in one sense, to expect an outcome is simply to assign

18 The border between interpersonal/participant and objective relations is actually a blurry one. Consider, for example, the way one might engage with someone whom one knows to be moved only by fairly self-interested reasons. In urging a certain policy on this person, one is wise to stick to the self-interested arguments and not to rely on appeals to altruism or a spirit of community. If one believes these self-interested arguments are among the good ones, one still relates to this person interpersonally. Perhaps, however, the engagement here is not as fully interpersonal as an engagement where one feels free to appeal to all of the reasons one considers relevant to the issue at hand. Thanks to Elizabeth Harman for urging me to clarify this point.

19 Wallace, *Responsibility and the Moral Sentiments*, 20.

a high probability to it. I of course think the kind of expectation he has in mind has more to it: it involves as well adopting a particular licensing stance toward the probability one assigns. This difference between Wallace and me will eventually prove important, but I will set it aside, for now. Wallace's crucial point for present purposes is that there is a kind of expectation that is not *interpersonal*. This way of expecting an outcome means seeing events "objectively," not as either amenable or beholden to reasons. By contrast, the kind of expectation Wallace puts at the heart of his account is interpersonal. To *normatively* expect something of person is to see her as both amenable and beholden to reasons. I believe there are two parallel kinds of hope. The subject of previous chapters was not strictly limited to interpersonal hope. It was, for the most part, parallel to the first kind of expectation just identified. But now I want to turn our attention to a second kind, a way of placing hope *in* people that presupposes their status as reasoners.

As we saw in chapter 1, one of the best entries into the difference between apersonal or non-normative expectation and hope is through the different feelings they involve. To expect an outcome is, *inter alia*, to see the outcome's probability as licensing a sense of what Miceli and Castelfranchi call "entitlement" to the outcome: anger if it fails to manifest, pleasure but not joy it if it does;[20] to hope for an outcome is, *inter alia*, to see the outcome's probability as licensing a feeling of anticipation (but not entitlement): disappointment if it fails to manifest, joy if it does. This is also a good route to the difference between the interpersonal or normative analogues of these attitudes. Normative expectation, as we've seen, is conceptually connected to the reactive attitudes. Normative hope, by contrast, is conceptually connected to a set of attitudes that are close siblings to the reactive attitudes. To get a feel for these feelings and how they compare with the reactive attitudes, consider the following set of cases. First, as a baseline, an unambiguous case of *normative expectation*:

> *Tailgater:* I live on a street off of a major road, right before an onramp to a highway. The turn onto my street is very sharp and requires slowing way down. I am extremely resentful of the many, many people who impatiently tailgate me as I approach my street. This is dangerous and obnoxious behavior, and they ought not do it.

To normatively expect people not to tailgate is to treat the principle expressed by the imperative, *Don't tailgate!* as a norm—a requirement or prohibition applicable to those people. It is also to be prepared to feel resentment toward tailgaters. That I treat this principle as a *norm* is also reflected in the fact that I am not prepared to feel gratitude toward people who leave a reasonable distance between their cars and mine; for that is, after all, simply what they

---

20   Miceli, "Hope: The Power of Wish and Possibility," 259–60.

should do, and they don't deserve any particular credit for it. So *Tailgater* contrasts with cases of *treating a principle as a principle of good (not necessarily required) behavior*, such as:

> *Thoughtful Child:* The father comes home and finds that his daughter, instead of going out with friends after school, as planned, came home, folded the laundry, and prepared dinner. She remembered he has a project deadline at the end of the week and thought he might need the evening hours for work. He is surprised and grateful, both for the help and for her thoughtfulness.

The father's gratitude marks his attitude toward some principle: *Act generously sometimes*, or *Occasionally sacrifice personal pleasure in order to support your family*, or even *Help out around the house more often than you are explicitly asked*. He does not treat the relevant principle as a *norm*; he would not have resented it if she had gone out after school instead, or if she had never done more than was asked of her. Actions in compliance with this principle are, as he sees it, *principles of good behavior*.

One might think this case is parasitic on normative expectation. One might think, that is, that normative expectation means being prone to not only resentment if the expectee violates a norm, but also gratitude if she exceeds it (within the limits set by other normative expectations). On this analysis, the father feels gratitude in virtue of the fact that the *supererogatory* principles of generosity and helping present ways of going above and beyond one of his normative expectations—perhaps, *Be a minimally decent contributor to the household*. He would feel resentment if his daughter never contributed, but he does not when she fails to go above and beyond what is required.

Matters are not always so clear-cut, however. Sometimes we do not feel grateful when people exceed our normative expectations. Wallace points out that we do not feel grateful for "supererogatory acts that do not benefit us in any way."[21] One might argue that, when one is not the beneficiary of a supererogatory act, one does not allege individual but impersonal authority, so one feels instead something like admiration, rather than gratitude. However, there are cases where people do allege individual authority with regard to a norm, and yet do not feel gratitude when the expectee goes beyond satisfying the norm. For example:

> *Unpleasant Boss:* Ebenezer is a real taskmaster. If Bob doesn't put in at least fifty hours a week, Ebenezer yells at him and accuses him of shirking his duties. The week prior to Christmas, Bob (who is a bit of a doormat) decides that, since what Ebenezer cares about most is work and profit, Bob will gift him with labor: he puts in seventy diligent, focused, productive

---

21 Wallace, *Responsibility and the Moral Sentiments*, 71.

hours, which brings in an unexpected boost in year's end profits. Ebenezer continues to be a nasty boss, and shows no sign of gratitude.

Ebenezer holds Bob to a norm of working at least fifty hours a week—this is evident in his expressed resentment of any less. He, being a stingy jerk, does not feel gratitude when Bob delivers more. Even if Ebenezer *ought* to feel gratitude, the absence of this feeling or a sense of its being warranted does not reveal that Ebenezer does not have a normative expectation of Bob. While it is true that we often do feel gratitude—and see it as warranted—when people exceed our normative expectations, our normative expectations do not depend on this truth.

As a final piece of evidence that gratitude is not conceptually tied to normative expectation in the same way as resentment, note that we are prone to feel gratitude to people who act according to certain principles, when we would also resent their failure to so act. Consider

> *Helpful Shopper*: Cyril has his arms full of grocery bags and is struggling to get his car open. He drops his keys on the ground just as a woman, unencumbered, walks past. She stops, picks up the keys, and asks him if would like her to open the car for him. He is grateful for her help, but he would also have resented it if she had walked past without stopping to help.

This is a very common sort of case. We feel appreciative when people do their jobs well, and feel grateful for even minor assistance; we even sometimes feel grateful to people who do what we believe are strict moral duties, like keeping a promise, refraining from cheating, or warning us of imminent danger. Yet we are not treating the principles governing such actions as supererogatory, because we also resent failures to do one's job well, be a minimally Good Samaritan, or uphold moral duties. On the face of it, we seem to treat such principles both as norms and as supererogatory. But this implies inconsistency: both seeing a principle as a requirement and seeing action in accordance with it as going above and beyond what is required.[22]

Adding the concept of normative hope to our repertoire allows an alternative interpretation of cases like *Helpful Shopper*, an interpretation that avoids attributing widespread inconsistency to our interpersonal attitudes. Gratitude and admiration are manifestations not of normative expectation, but of normative hope. Now let's consider a case that I believe most clearly

---

22 In a footnote, Wallace recognizes that "Gratitude is sometimes . . . appropriate in cases where no action that is morally exceptional has been performed—one might feel grateful toward a secretary who has served one dutifully for many years. What one feels grateful for, in a case of this sort, is loyalty or dependability or service over time (which might itself be exceptional)" ibid., 71. I take it that a one-off case like *Helpful Shopper* shows that this isn't a sufficient analysis of gratitude or of the conditions under which it is appropriate.

represents normative hope, one that turns our attention to disappointment rather than gratitude:

> *Lying Teenager*: A daughter tells her father she is spending the night at a friend's house. Instead, she goes to a frat party at the nearby university. The father finds out and, instead of getting angry, feels deeply *disappointed*. "You let me down," he says. "I'm disappointed in you."

There is no question that the father's disappointment is different from the disappointment we feel when an anticipated event fails to eventuate and that, more specifically, the former is *interpersonal*. He feels let down in virtue of his feeling that there were reasons for his daughter to be honest with him, reasons she ought to have taken into account, and that she instead ignored. This is disappointment *in* a person, rather than disappointment *at* the way the world has turned out.

Could this disappointment be just a variant of resentment, and this another case of normative expectation? I think not. I think there is a version of this case that belies this interpretation. Imagine that upon first learning of his daughter's deception, the father feels full-on reactive anger: *That little jerk! She knows better than that!* he thinks. But then he remembers that she is only fifteen years old. *She's been under enormous pressure lately. It's the end of the semester, and she's overwhelmed with work. Plus that friend of hers is being so mean to her, and she really doesn't know how to cope with it. I'm expecting too much of her,* he decides. *I shouldn't be so angry.*

This reasoning invokes classic Strawsonian "exempting" and "excusing" conditions.[23] The father has decided that his teenager is not a fully competent reasoner, and that she was facing extraordinarily challenging circumstances. He thereby decides that it is not strictly appropriate to hold her responsible for her action—she and her choice do not present apt targets for reactive feelings. Of course, he may nevertheless decide to respond to her *as if* she were a fully responsible agent, with the intention of "scaffolding" her into such agency; so he may act as if he is angry and resentful, and issue punishment. He may also decide that she is, after all, a *somewhat* competent reasoner, and not an *entirely* inappropriate target of the reactive attitudes, and so allow himself a modified resentment, along with its expression. The point remains, however, that he is committed to seeing full-blown resentment as inappropriate.

Not so with disappointment, however. Even after he reasons his way to seeing resentment, or at least full-blown resentment, as inappropriate, he may continue to think it is entirely legitimate for him to feel let down by his

---

23   Watson, "Responsibility and the Limits of Evil: Variations on a Strawsonian Theme" in his *Agency and Answerabilty*: 219–59.

daughter. He may think that she could have tried harder to get her priorities straight; that, if she had, she would not have pulled this stunt; and he may feel entirely let down by her failure. His stance is one that, unlike normative expectation, incorporates his daughter's status as an underdeveloped and challenged reasoner. The feeling of disappointment that manifests this stance thus accommodates this status. His stance is, like normative expectation, *sui generis*—it is its own irreducible way of relating to someone interpersonally. It is a way of treating a principle as worth aspiring to, without *insisting* on compliance.

I think the stance manifested in interpersonal disappointment is best understood as a kind of hope. Hope is, as I have analyzed it, structured in just the right way to incorporate the father's beliefs about his daughter's status as a reasoner. Non-normative hope involves a stance taken toward the probability one assigns to the hoped-for outcome, such that it licenses certain feelings and not others—in the case that the outcome does not eventuate, disappointment but not anger.[24] Normative hope involves a stance taken toward the capacities and/or situation of the agent about whom one hopes, such that they license certain feelings and not others—in the case that she does not act as one hopes, interpersonal disappointment but not reactive anger. To be precise, to normatively hope that a person will conform to a norm is to:

1 Be attracted to her conforming to the norm, in virtue of some set of features of this conformity;
2 Believe conforming to the norm is an achievable challenge for her. (For example, because her status as a reasoner is in some way compromised though developmentally open. Or, one might believe conformity to the norm is beyond an ordinary reasoner, but aspire on someone's behalf that they be more than ordinary, as we sometimes do with our leaders. And, finally, one might believe conformity is not beyond ordinary reasoners, but aspire on behalf of only select people, such as friends and loved ones).
3 See that status as licensing the transformation of one's attraction and the attractive features of conformity into reasons to feel interpersonal disappointment if she fails to conform, gratitude if she succeeds.

---

24 Non-normative hope means seeing the relevant probability as licensing certain forms of thought and planning, as well. For the purposes of examining normative hope, however, it is better to focus exclusively on feelings. This is for at least two reasons. First, the feelings of normative hope are the most clearly distinctive aspect of the attitude—the cases I am discussing make it clear that these feelings are sui generis, especially in relation to normative expectation. Second, it's not clear that imaginative exercises like fantasy and agential practices like planning are as essential to normative hope as they are to its non-normative counterpart. Just as it is possible to normatively expect someone to behave in a certain way without either dedicating much thought to or relying on it, it is possible to normatively hope without doing anything beyond standing ready to justify feelings of disappointment and gratitude in the appropriate circumstances.

4 Treat that attraction and those features as reasons for feeling inter-personal disappointment if she fails to conform, gratitude if she succeeds.

I would give a parallel analysis of normative expectation, such that my account diverges from Wallace's in an important way. Wallace argues that it is sufficient for normative expectation *either* that one sees reactive attitudes as warranted *or* that one is simply disposed to feel the reactive attitudes, without taking any position on their legitimacy or justification. On my view, both normative expectation and normative hope are necessarily justificatory stances: only the first of Wallace's two conditions is sufficient for normative expectation, and only a person who sees interpersonal disappointment as a legitimate response to a person's failure to act in accordance with a norm counts as normatively hoping for such action.

Wallace thinks normative expectation must be possible in the absence of any commitment to the legitimacy of the reactive attitudes, because otherwise we cannot "ascribe these emotions to people who find the emotion uncalled for from the perspective of the . . . demands they accept."[25] *Acceptance* of a norm is to be distinguished from the *internalization* of a norm.[26] Internalizing a norm is simply being disposed to act in conformity with it. Accepting a norm is, by contrast, what Wallace calls an "evaluative" state: "It involves a . . . tendency to adduce reasons that support the [norm], reasons that weigh with one for purposes of practical deliberation, and that one is prepared to call on to justify one's behavior and perhaps to address criticisms and recommendations to others."[27]

Wallace argues that normative expectation is different from either internalization or acceptance. But my analyses of normative hope and expectation make these stances into specific ways of accepting a norm. Normative hope involves the tendency to adduce reasons that support conformity to the norm; these reasons weigh with the hopeful person for purposes of practical deliberation about a certain way of feeling; and she is prepared to call on these reasons to justify her feeling. The parallel analysis of normative expectation would make it a closely related but distinct way of accepting a norm. So we should consider Wallace's objection to such approaches.

His primary target is John Rawls, who defines the reactive attitudes thus: "In general, it is a necessary feature of moral feelings, and part of what distinguishes them from the natural attitudes, that the person's explanation of

25 Wallace, *Responsibility and the Moral Sentiments*, 49.

26 Wallace takes these concepts from Alan Gibbard, but unpacks them in a more normative and less naturalistic way than Gibbard. For Gibbard's own theory, see his *Wise Choices, Apt Feelings: A Theory of Normative Judgment* (Cambridge, MA: Harvard University Press, 1990); and *Thinking How to Live* (Cambridge, MA: Harvard University Press, 2003).

27 Wallace, *Responsibility and the Moral Sentiments*, 41.

his experience invokes a moral concept and its associated principles. His account of his feeling makes reference to an acknowledged right or wrong."[28] Rawls's characterization of normative expectation, then, would be similar to mine, in that it would include a commitment to the justifiability of the relevant norm—the feelings that manifest the expectation are those that the expectant person would explain by appeal to the violation of a norm she genuinely accepts.

Wallace makes his case by focusing on what he calls "irrational guilt:" "It is notoriously the case that one can feel guilt without believing that one has really done anything wrong. We might express this by saying that one can feel guilt without believing that one has violated any demands that one *accepts*."[29] He points out that, not only do people sometimes feel guilty over behavior they see as perfectly legitimate—as in good old "Catholic guilt"—but also "the kinds of neurosis and anguish often associated with guilt in such cases presuppose that there is something one feels guilty about, some propositional object of one's emotional state."[30] I think, though, that both Rawls and I can accommodate these observations.

First Rawls. He develops his conception of the reactive attitudes—which he calls the "moral sentiments"—as part of his argument that, in a well-ordered society, where citizens have a well-developed sense of justice, stability is best promoted by a conception of justice as fairness. In such a society, he argues, people will develop through three stages with regard to the moral emotions. The children in a well-ordered society experience the "morality of authority," whereby they begin to internalize their beloved and trusted parents' fair judgments about their actions, and thereby experience "authority guilt" when they act in ways they know their parents will disapprove. They do not yet, however, have the concepts to (fully) understand norms or reasons, and so this feeling does not presuppose any sense of its own justifiability. As these children age, they begin to experience the "morality of associations," whereby they acquire a collection of sophisticated concepts and skills, which enables them to recognize and care about the claims of fellow association members (their family, school, union, or nation). The moral sentiments experienced at this stage are complex and have many familiar behavioral manifestations such as an inclination to reparation, and the willingness to apologize and concede to the appropriateness of punishment. They are still, however, dependent on the "natural attitudes" of love for and trust in one's fellow association members, for without these attachments, people in the stage of the morality of associations would not experience anything like guilt. Only in the final stage of development, the "morality of principles," do moral

28   John Rawls, *A Theory of Justice*, 421.
29   Wallace, *Responsibility and the Moral Sentiments*, 40.
30   Ibid., 47–48.

sentiments achieve independence from personal attachments. People who live with institutions and associations structured by the principles of justice come to care about the principles of justice and the ideal of the just person, for the sake of these principles and this ideal. When they experience guilt, the explanation is that they have violated the principles of justice, full stop. Rawls does emphasize that people's personal attachments intensify the moral sentiments experienced within the morality of principles, but he argues that the distinctly *moral* character of these sentiments is due to their noncontingent status.

For Rawls, then, if a person who grew up in a well-ordered society experienced guilt for an action she did not think violated the principles of justice, it would not be guilt "in the strict sense," but most likely authority guilt. This would be evident in various facts about her feelings and behavior: for example a reluctance to apologize, or a sense that punishment is not appropriate. Wallace suggests that Rawls thereby "goes too far in the direction of defining [guilt] in terms of its behavioral manifestations,"[31] but I don't think this is the right way to interpret the point. Even if moral guilt in the strict sense is a *sui generis* feeling, identifiable only by its occurrent presence, the fact remains that there are standard behaviors that mark it, and we should be skeptical that someone who exhibits none or almost none of the relevant behaviors really is experiencing the same feeling as someone who exhibits all of them.

We should also take seriously Rawls's emphasis on his account's relativity to the well-ordered society. (Wallace does acknowledge this emphasis in a footnote.[32]) We do not live in a well-ordered society, and it is extremely likely that our moral sentiments are not the rather rarified experiences Rawls discusses. When we feel guilt, even when it is guilt that approaches the "strict sense"—that is, even when it is guilt focused primarily on having violated a precept of right—it is probably a mélange of feelings consequent to our violation of principles we accept, our failure to live up to demands made by authority figures we love and trust, and the threat of punishment. It should come as no surprise, then, that it is difficult to distinguish, through introspection of our own experiences, strictly moral guilt from its developmental ancestors and closely related fears. Wallace has not found a special threat to Rawls's account, when he observes that "we frequently ascribe guilt to people who do not believe they have really done anything morally wrong"; and that "moreover, the kinds of neurosis and anguish often associated with guilt in such cases presuppose that there is something one feels guilty about, some propositional object of one's emotional state."[33] Wallace thinks the most plausible background account of neurotic guilt, for example, is that it

---

31   Ibid., 47.
32   Ibid., 47, n.42.
33   Ibid., 47–48.

presupposes the belief that one has violated precepts of right, *that are not demands one accepts*. But it is at least as plausible that the forms of guilt we want to call neurotic are the ancestors and relatives of strictly moral guilt, detached from their own appropriate circumstances, and even mistaken for strictly moral guilt.

So I take it Rawls has more than adequate resources to defend his view that reactive attitudes like guilt are conceptually connected to the judgment that the target has violated a norm one accepts. I don't want to endorse his developmental story in all its details—in particular, I am convinced neither that what Rawls calls the morality of principles is the endpoint on a progressive developmental scale, nor that we should withhold the label "moral" from the morality of association; Carol Gilligan's challenges to Piaget's and Kohlberg's work on moral development should make all of us cast a skeptical eye on such claims.[34] Nevertheless, I believe that: 1) It is methodologically valuable to parse out a form of guilt that presupposes the violation of endorsed or accepted norms; 2) This form of guilt and the related forms of resentment and indignation are at the heart of the interpersonal practice I have been calling "holding responsible"; and 3) There are developmental ancestors and contemporary relatives within our emotional repertoires that often accompany the strict sense of guilt and are readily mistaken for it. We can build on these points to support the analyses of normative expectation and hope I proposed above.

Two related observations in particular are important. First, it is possible to experience many of the elements of normative expectation and hope without arriving at the stances in their entirety. So, while a person raised in the Catholic Church who eventually rejects its doctrines might not fully normatively expect herself to conform to those doctrines, she might still find conformity a compelling or attractive idea. She might even see her status as a free agent as licensing feeling guilt at her failure to conform. As long as she maintains that she lacks sufficient reason to conform—especially that her conformist compulsions are no reason to conform—she does not count as fully normatively expecting herself to conform, and any "guilt" she actually experiences is less than the full-blown phenomenon. Second, these elements of normative expectation are recalcitrant, even the tendency to treat one's attractions to normative compliance as reasons. Although adopting an end or treating a consideration as a practical reason is a reason-responsive attitude or activity, it is not easy to resist the natural human propensity to rationalize compulsive behavior one knows is ill-supported by one's reasons. The same points apply to normative hope.

34 Carol Gilligan, *In a Different Voice: Psychological Theory and Women's Development* (Cambridge, MA: Harvard University Press. 1982). Rawls explicitly references the similarities between his theory of moral development and Kolhberg's (in *A Theory of Justice*, 404, n.8).

Moreover, guilt is the easy case for Wallace's argument. It is not as easy to think of cases of apparent resentment or indignation where one does not accept the relevant norms. It is certainly not impossible: I feel flashes of something like resentment at the natural world sometimes (*Stop raining!*); and one might catch oneself feeling rather *grrr* at a messy roommate, even if one thinks it would be hypocritical to expect her to be neater. But the phenomenology of such feelings is of something that is *self*-squelching. On Wallace's view, it requires a separate, external rejection of a norm to motivate us to squelch. Accounts like Rawls's and mine better fit the phenomenon: the inaptness of these feelings is built into them.

Having made the case for including a sense of justification within the stances of both normative expectation and normative hope, we can return now to gratitude. The normative hope that a person will uphold a norm, I have argued, is typically manifested in interpersonal disappointment when the person fails to uphold the norm.[35] It is also manifested in gratitude when the person upholds the norm.

Cases like *Unpleasant Boss* and *Helpful Shopper* show that gratitude does not track normative expectation. At first glance, it seems like gratitude is a reactive attitude that complements resentment, that it is what we feel when people exceed our normative expectations. But sometimes we don't feel gratitude when people exceed our normative expectations, and sometimes we feel gratitude when they only meet our expectations. This is because gratitude is the normative analogue of the joy we feel when our non-normative hopes are realized, rather than the "mere relief"[36] we feel when our non-normative expectations are satisfied. There are in fact no strong positive feelings conceptually tied to normative or non-normative expectation; the feelings of interpersonal demand and entitlement give way to feelings of satisfaction or relief with a quiet occurrent presence. There are, however, strong positive feelings conceptually tied to normative and non-normative hope: gratitude and impersonal joy, respectively.

The fact that we often feel gratitude when people exceed our normative expectations reveals not that gratitude is a feeling reserved for the supererogatory, to be defined in a way that is parasitic on resentment, but rather that we often adopt the stance of normative hope toward actions that we also view as supererogatory. In *Thoughtful Teenager*, the father's gratitude reflects something different from his expectation that she be an at least minimally contributing member of the houseful and his belief that she has done more than that; it reflects instead the fact that he *hopes* his daughter will be a thoughtful and generous person. His normative hope is a way of holding up principles of generous consideration as aspirational, principles there is reason for his

35 I discuss an exception, below, regarding normative hopes for supererogatory action.
36 Miceli, "Hope . . . ," 261.

daughter to strive to embody in her deliberation and choices. (He may *also* think of such principles as supererogatory—but that is not what his gratitude tells us.) In *Lying Teenager*, by contrast, he treats the principle of honesty and forthrightness as aspirational, because he sees it as too challenging to be fully normative for his daughter—though for a more fully developed agent, it would be fully normative and his stance would be normative expectation rather than hope.

In *Helpful Shopper*, we see an interesting situation where Cyril both normatively hopes for and normatively expects conformity to the same principle. This combination of attitudes might seem strange, but normative hope and normative expectation are not necessarily in either conceptual or psychological tension with each other. It is possible to simultaneously see a person's status or situation as a reasoner in both hopeful and expectant ways: thus one stands ready to justify feeling both disappointed and resentful if the person in question fails to meet one's hope and expectation, and both grateful and satisfied if she meets them. There are a number of reasons one might adopt this two-fold attitude.

In *Lying Teenager*, the father adopts the attitude of normative hope because he sees his daughter as a compromised or developmentally incomplete reasoner, not necessarily up to the challenges her situation poses. This rationale precludes also adopting the attitude of normative expectation. But there are other views one might have of a person that leave the space for both normative hope and normative expectation. In *Helpful Shopper*, the likely view is that, although the average passerby is both beholden to a norm requiring assistance and capable of meeting that norm, there is also something about the situation that makes basic decency something to aspire to: in particular, we live in a pretty selfishly-oriented society, where "look out for number one" is actually considered a legitimate principle of action, in at least some situations. So while we are not inclined to excuse selfish behavior, simple generosities can be normatively surprising—it is not merely that such acts are statistically unlikely, but that they go against some strong normative notions that thread through our culture. Thus there is something especially admirable about shaking off these notions and meeting our obligations of unsolicited kindness. That, anyway, is the implication of our usual interpersonal feelings.

Hope for the Vicious

An apparently simple case like *Helpful Shopper* reveals that our ordinary interpersonal attitudes are complex: we often simultaneously hold people fully responsible—and thereby treat them as fully free rational agents—and recognize the challenges that are inherent in being an empirically embedded individual, the obstacles, that is, to effectively exercising that free agency. In the cases we have seen so far, the obstacles are external to the individual. But we also sometimes adopt the same duality of stance when we believe the obstacles are *internal*; that is, when it is a person's own character that interferes with her deliberation and makes her prone to making the wrong choice. Even while we fully normatively expect the vicious or corrupt to do what is right, we see that it is unlikely that they will, and we normatively hope that they will overcome their own shortcomings. Meeting our normative expectations is, for the vicious, something to aspire to. This attitude has the potential to be a form of encouragement, a condemnation, or both.

The story that first suggested to me the idea of normative hope contains an example of hope as a form of condemnation. It comes from David Dow's book, *Autobiography of an Execution*, where he tells the story of the legal scramble to save the life of his client, Walter Buckley. Ten hours before Buckley's scheduled execution, Dow's staff at the Texas Defender Service found decisive evidence that Buckley was retarded. Buckley's previous attorney had failed to raise this evidence because, according to him, "Buckley just didn't seem that slow."[37] Dow and his colleagues raced to write their claim for the Texas state court, presenting the proof that Buckley had dropped out of school in the 7th grade, had scored between 53 and 59 on three IQ tests, had never been able to live by himself, and had been deemed retarded by three doctors (including one employed by the state)—and explaining why the court was seeing this proof only now. As they prepared to email it from Houston to their Austin office, where someone could deliver it to the courthouse, their computer system crashed. What happened next is beyond belief.

They called the court near four pm to explain the situation, and were informed the court would close at five. By the time they finally got the computers back up and printed the lengthy claim—at the time, the Texas state court did not accept electronic filings—it was a few minutes past five. They called the court to say they were coming to deliver the claim, and were told by a clerk that the court closed at five. They drove over and banged on the door, but no one answered. Dow describes their last-ditch effort to save Buckley:

> We had a problem. It was almost five thirty, and the papers that we had been working on for the Supreme Court were based on the assumption that we had lost in state court, not on the assumption that we had never managed to get anything filed in that court. We couldn't file an appeal from the state court's decision, because there was no state court decision. I won't bore you with the details of why this is a complicated problem, but it is. So I quickly wrote something up, asking the Supreme Court to issue a stay of execution, promising the justices that we would get something

37 David R. Dow, *The Autobiography of an Execution* (New York: Twelve, 2010), 211. Copyright 2010 David R. Dow.

filed in the state court the following day. I knew as we were emailing it to the Court at minutes before six that it had all kinds of technical legal problems, but I hoped they would not matter, that what the justices would focus on was the fact that Buckley had an IQ score somewhere in the mid-50s. But hope is an impotent indulgence. One day soon, I swear, I am going to give up on it completely. The justices unanimously turned us down.[38]

Dow condemns hope throughout the book, which indeed documents a life dedicated to a practice any reasonable person would call hopeless. He says he tries continually to take away all hope from his clients, to convince them from the start that all of his efforts are destined to failure, and that their executions are inevitable. He also repeatedly lambasts his own hopes as foolish, pointless and, as above, impotent. His reason seems to be that it is so painful to have one's hopes crushed. He says of his clients that his efforts to stamp out hope derive from self-interest: "It is easier to tell someone who is prepared to die that he is about to die."[39] Of his own hopes, his remarks are sometimes suggestive of a desire to give up his practice entirely, but is clear that this desire does not run very deep—his desire to stop hoping that justices will look past legal technicalities to the moral heart of a case; that a corrupt judge will, just this once, do what is right; that the Board of Governors will see the significance of their responsibility in refusing yet another stay; that the prosecution will put their humanity ahead of their state-designated roles is not a desire to stop defending death row inmates, but a desire to stop *feeling* so much, to be less emotionally invested in each case and, thereby, to find the job a bit more bearable.

One might protest that, without hope, Dow wouldn't have the motivation to pursue his line of work. I doubt this is true, though. His sense of duty is more than adequate. What I do think, though, is that at least some of the hopes I've listed are normative hopes, and that they embody Dow's moral convictions regarding the people holding up a morally bankrupt system. These people are, by the light of Dow's hope, rather like teenagers—except that it is their vice rather than their underdeveloped brains compromising their choices. This rationale for normative hope—that a person is capable of acting rightly but compromised by her own moral failings—is not only consistent with normative expectation, but even calls for it. (Assuming she is capable of improving herself and thereby responsible for her moral failings.) So it only makes sense that Dow's response to the Court's failing is both deep interpersonal disappointment and powerful indignation: when Gary berates himself for the IT failure, Dow says, "Pal, there is a long list of people whose fault it is, including nine in Austin and nine more in Washington, and your

38   Ibid., 214–15.
39   Ibid., 15.

name is not on it."[40] There is, as he says, plenty of blame to go around, and he does not hesitate to assign it, or to feel the righteous anger to which he is entitled.

Reactive anger and indignation roil throughout the book. A deep feeling of sadness also pervades—sadness of course at the death of Dow's clients at the hands of the state, but also a profound disappointment in the society that allows such a system to persist, and even celebrates it.[41] Even if I have mis-read Dow, and the hopes he expresses and denounces are all non-normative hopes for non-agential events to unfold in a way that supports his project, and he feels none of the interpersonal disappointment I have been discuss-ing, it is certainly plausible that someone in his position could entertain the normative hopes and feel the disappointment I am attributing to him. This disappointment contains or implies a multi-part judgment about the people who uphold the system: That something about them makes it unlikely they will do the right thing; that it is something for which they are culpable or accountable—i.e., it is not an exempting or excusing condition; and that it is possible for them to overcome this internal obstacle to right action.

This judgment amounts to a judgment that doing the right thing is, for these people, an achievable challenge. In entertaining the normative hope that the justices will look past legal technicalities to the moral heart of the case, one sees the possibility that they will overcome their culpable moral limitations as enough to license interpersonal disappointment if they fail to do so. And, if my analysis of normative hope is right, also gratitude in the event they do. This might strike many as implausible. But in fact it is true to the actual moral psychology we see in such situations. The fact is that we *do* often feel grateful when corrupt people do the right thing for the right rea-sons. It's more than a feeling of relief; it is the interpersonal analogue.

Is it objectionable to invest normative hope in the vicious? One might think so, insofar as one objects to feeling grateful to the vicious for overcom-ing their vice. But, as long as we continue to normatively expect the vicious to improve, such gratitude has quite an edge to it: it is not a sign that we have let someone off the hook, or that we treat righteousness as supererogatory for corrupt souls; instead, it is a sign that we think so poorly of their characters that we see righteous behavior as a special challenge for them. After all, a relatively virtuous person should be insulted, if one says to her, "I really hope you'll do the right thing here," or, "I'm so grateful you did."[42]

---

40 Ibid., 215.

41 Consider the enthusiastic applause that greeted Texas Governor Rick Perry's execution record during a September 2011 Republican presidential primary debate.

42 Also worth considering is the possibility that in many cases of investing hope in the vi-cious, we are investing an attitude that presupposes the analogue of representative, rather than individual authority, so that what we feel is not gratitude, but a "vicarious" feeling of something like admiration.

Summary

Hope in general is not often discussed by philosophers, particularly secular philosophers outside of the phenomenological tradition. In the first four chapters of this book, I aimed to persuade that this neglect is a pity. Hope is a distinctive attitude that relies on sophisticated agential capacities, and through which we incorporate our subrational motivations into our rational agency. Hope also has a complex and important role—both contingent and, in the case of unimaginable hope, intrinsic—to play in our struggles with life's trials. Normative hope receives even less attention than hope more broadly construed—indeed, I am unaware of any philosopher who has identified it as a distinctive attitude. Once we turn our sights on a certain class of interpersonal feelings and attitudes, however, I think it is clear that there is a practice closely related to holding people responsible that is best understood as a mode of investing hope in people. When we invest hope in people, we stand ready to feel and to justify feeling disappointment in the event that they fail to act as we hope and gratitude when they succeed. Investing hope in a person is thus different from, though compatible with, holding her responsible through the disposition to feel the reactive attitudes; to invest hope in a person is to relate some norm to her aspirationally, to hold it up to her as something with which she has decisive reason to comply, while acknowledging the challenges she faces, externally or internally. Investing hope is a practice that is both important and valuable, for consequentialist reasons: it can be an essential part of scaffolding a person's developing agency; it can be a form of condemnation that may both promote the rehabilitation of the vicious and deter the potentially vicious. More fundamentally, though, it is a practice like holding people responsible, that is intrinsically valuable for the meaning it constitutes in human relationships.

Human Passivity, Agency, and Hope

The scenarios that originally inspired this investigation point to a quasi-dilemma that people often associate with hope. This quasi-dilemma takes on slightly different casts in different circumstances: in a medical setting, where hoped-for outcomes are largely beyond the hopeful person's control, people worry about how to avoid "false" hope without losing all hope; in a political setting, where politicians invoke hope in order to draw support, people instead worry about being led down the primrose path, and wonder if the alternative to cynicism is losing touch with reality. Setting aside such variations, the quasi-dilemma is essentially about the challenge of finding a hope that is supportive or motivational but that does not require, for its maintenance, manipulation, deception, or detachment from reality. It is common to think that meeting this challenge means following a blanket rule that directs us to hope and encourage others to hope only for somewhat probable outcomes. Call this *the rule against improbable hope.*

I have argued that a principle bearing some resemblance to the rule against improbable hope is true: it is irrational to form or maintain a hope based on the belief that the hoped-for outcome is either more or less probable than one's evidence indicates. Subjective probability estimates should be based on one's evidence, or perhaps the evidence one would take into account if one were fully epistemically responsible. But we must not take this rather narrow requirement for more than it is. The advocates of the rule against improbable hope mean to rule out hopes for extremely improbable outcomes. And, at least rationally speaking, the only considerations that can rule out such hopes are *practical* ones.

That, I take it, is how the advocates of the rule against improbable hope conceive it: as a *prudential* recommendation. That is, they think improbable hopes are potentially tragic wastes of energy and time. One important result of my proposed analysis of hope is that restricting hopes to somewhat probable outcomes is neither necessary nor sufficient for practical rationality. Even some very strong hopes for extremely improbable outcomes—hopes that dominate our thoughts, feelings, and plans—may further our rational ends. They may sustain us through trials that would otherwise cause us to collapse or self-destruct; they may help us find means to elusive ends; they may simply make life more pleasant by bolstering a cheerful sensibility. Conversely, some hopes for moderately probable hopes may sabotage our pursuit of rational ends. They may cause us to lose touch with reality; they may substitute fantasy for the enactment of effective plans; they may lead us to overvalue hoped-for outcomes.

These possibilities are to some degree visible even from the perspective of the orthodox definition of hope. Desire—even conceived along the lines of subrational attraction—disposes us to imaginative engagement with the desired outcome and the circumstances in which it might be realized; it also turns our attention away from potentially despair-inducing information. However, the full force of hope's potential (positive and negative) influences on deliberation, motivation, and the ability to abide a trial becomes clear only once we recognize that hope is a way of taking up or "incorporating" the probability estimate and attraction of the orthodox definition into our rational agency. The hopeful agent not only engages with the hoped-for outcome in imagination, not only plans on the outcome, and not only focuses on hope-supporting information: she also treats such modes of thought and attention as rationally justified in virtue of the outcome's probability and attractive features. This is what distinguishes the hopeful person from another who has the same beliefs and desires with regard to the same outcome, but either resists hope, or even falls into despair.

Let me emphasize this last point. Although my argumentative strategy in developing the incorporation analysis was to focus on cases of "hoping against hope," this was only because it is in such cases that the distinctive aspects of hope are most salient. I do not believe these cases are either "fringe" cases or deserving of their own category separate from more prosaic hopes. Even the most prosaic hope involves treating the hoped-for outcome's probability and desirable features as justifying reasons for hopeful thoughts, feelings, and plans. This aspect of hope is simply not particularly noticeable in a prosaic hope, because the hopeful person's relatively high degree of confidence or minor degree of attraction generates few of these hopeful activities. Nevertheless, she is, in virtue of her hope, poised to justify such activities by appeal to the probability of and attractive features of the outcome for which she hopes.

Moving to the incorporation analysis of hope means abandoning a monist account of human action—such as Humean pure nonrationalism or Scanlonian pure rationalism—for a dualist account that attributes to us both nonrational and rational forms of motivation. The analysis requires rational motivational representations to capture the fact that the hopeful person stands ready to offer practical justifications for her rational activities; and it requires nonrational (or, as I prefer to say, *sub*-rational) motivational representations to capture the specific content of these hopeful justifications: the hopeful person is poised to offer justifications that include an appeal to the hoped-for outcome's attractive features and thus also, at least in the background but perhaps also explicitly, an appeal to the fact that she is attracted to the outcome in virtue of those features.

This move is, I believe, salutary for the philosophy of psychology in general and the philosophy of emotional attitudes in particular. With regard to emotional attitudes, a dualist account of our motivational resources provides the resources necessary for plausible, unified syndrome analyses. As I noted in the introduction, syndrome analyses—whereby emotional attitudes are conceived as complexes of feelings, motives, and perhaps judgments—have a great deal of intuitive appeal, because our experience of these attitudes includes such a complexity of elements. Loving someone, for example, involves feelings of pleasure in her presence and in the awareness of her flourishing, pain in the absence of these things, as well as substantial motives to pursue intimacy with her and to promote her flourishing. However, such analyses do not always hang together in a philosophically convincing way; they lack a unifying element or principle to explain why their various constituents present together. If, however, we admit into our psychology a capacity to reflect on feelings and attractions and to choose or refuse to treat them as practical reasons, we have a plausible unifying element. This is the capacity I have been calling the capacity to "incorporate" considerations into our rational agency.

Consider love. Drawing on the resources I have developed in relation to hope, we might conceive of love as both a passivity and an activity. Its passive aspects are, first, the feelings that give rise to certain subrational attractions. When we love a person, we (paradigmatically) find both her proximity and her flourishing pleasurable, her absence and her suffering painful. Because of these feelings, we become attracted to having her near and to contributing to her flourishing, and we find the counterparts of these outcomes aversive. Then, when this passive side of love develops into love in its fullest sense, we actively adopt the ends of being near to the beloved, and of contributing to her flourishing. These become active projects, exercises of our agency. I say love is a way of "incorporating" certain feelings and attractions into one's rational agency, because the lover treats them as practical reasons. She also, of course, treats the features of the beloved that produce these feelings and attractions as reasons: love is not exclusively self-centered, on this account. But a crucial element of love is *endorsing* the way one feels about the beloved, and how appealing and attractive one finds her and her flourishing. Such a conception explains why the particular feelings and motives of love hang together. The loving agent selectively incorporates certain attractions into her maxims, thereby *creating* a syndrome, an organized and unified collection of those maxims, attractions, and the feelings generating them. Thus, I think the sort of analysis I have developed in this book, with regard to hope, may serve as a general model for many emotional attitudes.

More generally speaking, moving to a dualist account of human action produces better accommodations for the variety of experiences of the reflective deliberating agent. We can be drawn to things in a conceptually simple way, and we are also capable of endorsing or rejecting both the features of things that attract us and the fact of our attraction as practical reasons. We can allow our attractions to move us by representing them as practical reasons, and we can resist them by refusing to represent them in this way. The suggestion above, that love is both a passivity and an activity, is a specification of a general truth about our experience of the world and ourselves in it: we are moved by things, and we are also movers.

The lines we draw with respect to the conditions of responsibility reflect this truth. Insofar as we see a person as an active mover in the world, taking up her own attractions and the things that attract her as practical reasons, we think it appropriate to expect her to be able to justify her actions. Insofar as we see her as passively moved by the world, we withhold this expectation (the exception being that we often hold people responsible for failing to train their capacity to be passively moved). And this brings us to normative hope.

Normative hope is not, precisely, a way of holding people responsible. It is, however, a way of relating to them as active movers in the world—more specifically, as active movers capable of aspirational rather than requisite self-improvement and self-maintenance. Some normative hopes are based on the recognition that not everyone is capable of properly evaluating or controlling the passive part of her nature at all times. The hopes we place in developing agents, such as teenagers, and impermanently damaged agents, such as the vicious or corrupt, are ways of recommending without insisting on improvement. We recommend, specifically, better recognition of and responsiveness to norms and the reasons underwriting them. This is, in part, to recommend better evaluative judgment regarding their own passive nature and, thereby, better control over that nature.

Other normative hopes are based on the belief that some people can achieve specially refined evaluation of and control over their passive natures. The hopes we place in people, such as our leaders and our friends, in virtue of their special relationships to us, and not in virtue of their underdeveloped or damaged agency, are ways of asking without demanding that they become or continue to be specially admirable, loveable, or respectable people. And this is, in part, to request that they exercise specially refined evaluative judgment of and control over their passive natures.

This book has explored two faces of hope: the impersonal hopes we place in the non-agential world and the normative hopes we place in agents. Impersonal hopes are a crucial way we bring our active capacity of practical rationality to bear on the facts that we are sensuous, desirous—i.e., passive—creatures with serious epistemic and agential limits. Indeed, by investing hope in attractive but uncertain outcomes, we not only bring our agency to bear on our passivity, we build this passivity into our agency. Normative hopes are a crucial way we aspire on behalf of others, and on our own behalf, to be better agents—more sensitive and responsive to interpersonal norms, and more skilled at determining when and how our passive natures should influence our actions. Throughout this book, I have urged skepticism about standard tropes regarding the power and value of hope. I have also, however, argued for a deeper and philosophically more interesting role for hope in our psychologies, whereby hope is a unifying capacity, joining our rational and more animal natures.

CPSIA information can be obtained
at www.ICGtesting.com
Printed in the USA
JSHW021148250622
27508JS00002B/107